A HANDLE ON HOMOPHONES

HOMOPHONES MADE EASY THROUGH RHYMES AND VERSES

by

GENEVIEVE FARRELL

WITH ILLUSTRATIONS BY KIRAN MEHDI

ORIGINAL WRITING

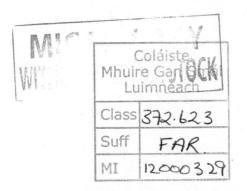
© 2011 Genevieve Farrell

Illustrations by Kiran Mehdi

978-1-908282-82-8

A CIP catalogue for this book is available from the National Library.

Published by Original Writing Ltd., Dublin, 2011.

Printed by Clondalkin Group, Clonshaugh, Dublin 17

Foreword

A HANDLE ON HOMOPHONES has been written to improve pupils' knowledge, comprehension and spelling of a wide range of common homophones (for example, *their, they're, there* and *to, two, too*) in the English language.

A HANDLE ON HOMOPHONES is a resource to facilitate teachers in teaching homophones to pupils. It aims to enable pupils to differentiate between a specified number of homophones used on a daily basis in the home, at school and outside the home, school, etc. through the fun medium of poetry. Through reading, listening to and writing rhymes and verses containing homophones, pupils' recognition, identification and learning of homophones is made easier. This book is aimed at middle and upper primary pupils of age range 8-12 years and its variety of practical lessons makes it suitable for mainstream, special needs and EAL pupils.

A HANDLE ON HOMOPHONES includes:

- Thirty relevant homophone poems containing elements of rhythm and rhyme
- High-interest, practical and enjoyable lessons
- Clear definitions of each homophone and examples
- Table of curriculum links, linking the activities to the English Language Curriculum for Ireland
- Teachers notes and answers to questions

A HANDLE ON HOMOPHONES provides the opportunity for pupils to not only enhance their knowledge, comprehension and spelling of homophones but also to engage with and write in a wide variety of poetry on a regular basis and to explore new interests and perspectives through reading poetry. The activities provided in this book cover many of the English language objectives in all four curriculum strands for Third, Fourth, Fifth and Sixth class.

CONTENTS

Information for teachers

Definition of a homophone: A homophone is one of a group of words pronounced in the same way but differing in meaning or spelling or both, for example, *bear* and *bare*.

A HANDLE ON HOMOPHONES is a very convenient and easily accessible copy-master for teachers and pupils. It consists of 30 homophone poems with accompanying teachers notes and pupil activity pages. All of the activity pages contain 6 individual exercises which are linked to the oral, writing and reading strand units of the English Language Curriculum for Ireland. Each poem has been written to clearly demonstrate the difference between a number of common homophones in the English language.

Activity pages

The activity pages in this book are clearly set out with exercises 1 (oral activity) and 6 (Writing and Reading activity) having the same format and both included for each poem. Exercises 2 – 5 contain a mixture of oral, writing and both reading and writing activities.

A) Oral activities
- Pupils listen to each poem being read aloud by their teacher
- Pupils practise reading each poem aloud
- Pupils observe tone of voice, gestures and facial expressions by their teacher and each other
- Pupils compare and contrast each other's tone of voice, gestures and facial expressions as they read each poem aloud
- Pupils describe their reaction to each poem
- Pupils respond to questions by their teacher on the poem

B) *Writing activities*

- Pupils write their own sentences including each homophone
- Pupils unscramble sentences containing homophones
- Pupils find homophones in a wordsearch

C) *Reading and Writing activities*

- Pupils match sentences containing homophones
- Pupils fill in the blanks using the correct homophones
- Pupils complete true or false statements/sentences containing homophones
- Pupils find the mistakes in sentences or in a short passage containing homophones

D) *Writing and Reading activities*

- Pupils write their own poem using either one of the homophones mentioned in each poem or all of the homophones mentioned
- Pupils read and recite their poem
- Pupils write about their favourite moment, an exciting character and what they liked about a poem they have listened to

The poems are set out in alphabetical order (as seen in the table of contents) and teachers may choose to follow the table of contents beginning with the teaching of the first set of homophones, *Allowed, Aloud* or they may begin with a set of homophones from the table of contents with which pupils are experiencing difficulty/displaying poor knowledge, comprehension etc. ,for example, *Your, You're*. Teachers should begin with the oral activities (exercise 1 and occasionally 2) for each poem and then allow pupils to work through the varying reading and writing activities. The final more challenging activity to be carried out should be the writing and reading activities, exercise 6.

Curriculum Links

A Handle on Homophones is a book for 8-12 year-olds. It covers many of the oral, writing and reading content objectives from the four strands of the English Language Curriculum for Ireland.

STRAND	STRAND UNIT	CLASS	CONTENT OBJECTIVES
Receptiveness to language	Oral	3rd & 4th	• Become increasingly aware of gesture, facial expressions, tone of voice, audibility and clarity of enunciation in communicating with others
		5th & 6th	• Be continually aware of the importance of gesture, facial expression, tone of voice, audibility and clarity of enunciation in communicating with others
	Writing	3rd & 4th	• Receive and give positive responses to writing
		3rd & 4th, 5th & 6th	• Observe the teacher modelling different writing genres (poems)
	Reading	3rd & 4th	• Refine his/her listening skills through hearing the teacher read aloud
		5th & 6th	• Engage with an increasing range of narrative, expository and representational text
Competence and confidence in using language	Oral	3rd & 4th	• Play synonym and antonym games
		5th & 6th	• Understand the functions and know the names of the parts of speech: *noun, verb, pronoun, preposition, etc.*
	Writing	3rd & 4th	• Use a range of aids and strategies to improve his/her command of spelling: *dictionaries, word searches, word lists, etc.*
		5th & 6th	• Observe the conventions of grammar, punctuation and spelling in his/her writing • Take part in co-operative writing activities: *writing and publishing poetry*
	Reading	3rd & 4th	• Engage with a wide variety of poetry and verse on a regular basis
		5th & 6th	• Read widely as an independent reader a more challenging range of materials, including poems

Developing cognitive abilities through language	Oral	3rd & 4th	• Learn how to use the basic key questions Why? How? Where? When? What? What if?
		5th & 6th	• Use the basic key questions and checking questions as a means of extending knowledge
	Reading	3rd & 4th	• Explore new interests and perspectives through reading poetry
		5th & 6th	• Listen to, read, learn, recite and respond to a challenging range of poetry • Use comprehension skills
	Writing	5th & 6th	• Write in a wide variety of genres: *poetry*
Emotional and imaginative development through language	Oral	3rd & 4th	• Discuss favourite moments, important events and exciting characters in a poem • Discuss reactions to poems • Experience and enjoy playful aspects of language: *composing rhymes and verses*
		5th & 6th	• Express individual responses to poems
	Writing	3rd & 4th	• Create/write poems
		5th & 6th	• Express in writing and analyse his/her reaction to poems
	Reading	3rd & 4th	• Extend and develop his/her responses to increasingly challenging reading material
		5th & 6th	• Respond to poetry through discussion and writing

Allowed, Aloud

Teachers Notes

Before the lesson

The teacher should have a list of examples and demonstrate how we use gesture, tone of voice and facial expressions in our everyday lives.

The lesson

1) Write the words *allowed* and *aloud* on the whiteboard and elicit knowledge from pupils of each word. Looking at exercise 1, explain to pupils that they are going to listen to you reading aloud a poem called *Allowed, Aloud* and try to recall from the poem the difference in meaning and spelling between each word.

2) Refer pupils to the *Explanation of each word* section at the top of the first activity page for further explanation and examples. Invite pupils to give their own examples.

3) Discuss with the pupils common gestures, tones of voice and facial expressions that we use.

4) Pupils listen to you reading the poem aloud a second time and then discuss your tone of voice, gestures and facial expressions.

5) Individually or in pairs, pupils practise reading the poem aloud and note each reader's tone of voice, gestures and facial expressions.

6) Pupils discuss their reaction to the poem.

7) Individually or in pairs, pupils complete fill in the blanks exercise. (no.2)

8) Individually or in pairs, pupils unscramble sentences containing both homophones learned. (exercise 3)

9) Pupils write their own sentences including each homophone. (exercise 4)

10) Individually or in pairs, pupils complete true or false exercise. (no.5)

11) Pupils write their own poem using either one or both homophones (exercise 6 with b) being more challenging!). The poem should be at least 4 lines in length and does not have to rhyme. Invite pupils to read and recite their poem. Pupils then pick one poem they have listened to and write about their favourite moment in it, an exciting character and what they liked about the poem.

Any of the above exercises 2-6 could be given as homework exercises.

Answers

4) – 6) Teacher check

7) Exercise 2: a) allowed; b) aloud; c) allowed; d) aloud; e) allowed; f) aloud.

8) Exercise 3: 1) We were allowed to have one slice of cake. 2) She read the instructions aloud for everyone to hear. 3) You are not allowed to speak aloud in this room.

9) Exercise 4: Teacher check

10) Exercise 5: 1) false; 2) true; 3) false; 4) true.

11) Exercise 6: Teacher check

Pupils could display their poems on the classroom wall(s).

Allowed, Aloud

'You're not *allowed* in there!'
a voice cried *aloud*.
'It's too dangerous for you.
You may get lost in the crowd!'

'Am I *allowed* to stay
with my friend?'
'If your homework is done
from beginning to end,'
my Mum spoke *aloud*
beside Mrs O' Dowd.

No speaking *aloud* in
this library please.
Not one sound *allowed* -
not as much as a breeze!

'No-one is *allowed* to
remove this cable,'
the teacher read *aloud*
from his wooden table.

Allowed, Aloud

Explanation of each word:

Allowed = the past tense of the verb allow meaning to permit (to do something).
Example: Mum *allowed* me to stay up until nine o'clock.

Aloud = an adverb meaning in a normal voice or in a spoken voice.
Example: He read *aloud* the first verse of the poem.

Exercise 1
Oral activity

1) Listen to your teacher reading the poem aloud.
What do you notice about your teacher's tone of voice?
What kinds of gestures and facial expressions is your teacher using?
2) Practise reading the poem aloud. Listen to each reader's tone of voice.
Look at the readers' gestures and facial expressions.
Are they the same or different?
3) Discuss your reaction to the poem with your teacher and class. What do you like about the poem?

Exercise 2
Reading and Writing activity

Read the poem and then see if you can fill in the blanks using *allowed* or *aloud*:

a) You are not _____ to leave this building.
b) She enjoys reading _____ in class.
c) They were only _____black tea and one slice of toast.
d) The man spoke _____ from the top table.
e) Do you think we'll be _____ to go home at 12pm?
f) Would you like to read your letter _____?

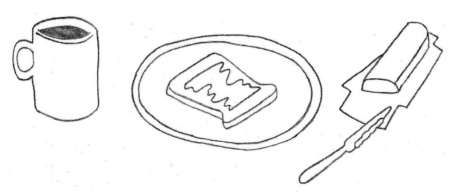

Exercise 3

Writing activity

Can you unscramble the following sentences?
(Remember to use a capital letter and full stop or question mark!):

1. to one cake of allowed were have slice we

_____

_____

2. aloud for hear to instructions she the everyone read

_____

_____

3. room are to this not speak in allowed you aloud

_____

_____

Exercise 4
Writing activity

Write your own sentences and include *allowed* in the first one, *aloud* in the second one and *allowed* and *aloud* in the last one:

1. (allowed)

_____

_____

2. (aloud)

_____

_____

3. (allowed, aloud)

_____

_____

Exercise 5
Reading and Writing activity

True or False:
1) He is not aloud to say anything about it._____
2) Why were you not allowed inside?_____
3) Project your voice as you read allowed._____
4) "Please help me!" he cried aloud._____

Exercise 6
Writing and Reading activity

1) Write your own poem using either:

a) the word *allowed* or *aloud*
> or
b) both words *allowed* and *aloud*

_____

_____

_____

_____

_____

_____

_____

_____

_____

2) Read and recite your poem to your partner and then to your class.

3) Pick one poem you have listened to and discuss your favourite moment in it.
Tell about an exciting character in the poem.
Write what you liked about the poem.

_____

_____

_____

_____

_____

_____

_____

_____

_____

_____

Bear, Bare

Teachers Notes

Before the lesson

The teacher should have a list of examples and demonstrate how we use gesture, tone of voice and facial expressions in our everyday lives.

The lesson

1) Write the words *bear* and *bare* on the whiteboard and elicit knowledge from pupils of each word. Looking at exercise 1, explain to pupils that they are going to listen to you reading aloud a poem called *Bear, Bare* and try to recall from the poem the difference in meaning and spelling between each word.
2) Refer pupils to the *Explanation of each word* section at the top of the first activity page for further explanation and examples. Invite pupils to give their own examples.
3) Discuss with the pupils common gestures, tones of voice and facial expressions that we use.
4) Pupils listen to you reading the poem aloud a second time and then discuss your tone of voice, gestures and facial expressions.
5) Individually or in pairs, pupils practise reading the poem aloud and note each reader's tone of voice, gestures and facial expressions.
6) Pupils discuss their reaction to the poem.
7) Ask pupils to answer orally, questions 1-5 on the poem (to check recall) without referring to the poem. (exercise 2)
8) Individually or in pairs, pupils complete find the mistakes exercise. (no.3)
9) Individually or in pairs, pupils match sentences containing each homophone learned.(exercise 4)
10) Pupils write their own sentences including each homophone. (exercise 5)
11) Pupils write their own poem using either one or both homophones (exercise 6 with b) being more challenging!). The poem should be at least 4 lines in length and does not have to rhyme. Invite pupils to read and recite their poem. Pupils then pick one poem they have listened to and write about their favourite moment in it, an exciting character and what they liked about the poem.

Any of the above exercises 3-6 could be given as homework exercises.

Answers

4) – 6) Teacher check
7) Exercise 2: 1) He was too busy scratching his head. 2) Moving his head from side to side and then rolling on the ground; 3) A cute baby bear appeared from behind the bare tree. 4) huddles; 5) scratch.
8) Exercise 3: a) I'm not afraid of that big, ugly bear. b) You can tell that it's winter because all the trees are bare. c) They couldn't bear to lose another game. d) Julia cannot find her new teddy bear.
9) Exercse 4: a) A baby bear is called a cub. b) She can't bear to look at it. c) The trees were bare after the storm. d) We saw a huge bear in the jungle. e) Our kitchen was quite bare after we cleared it out.
10) Exercise 5: Teacher check
11) Exercise 6: Teacher check

Pupils could display their poems on the classroom wall(s).

Bear, Bare

I see a big, brown *bear*
by a very *bare* tree.
Too busy scratching his head,
he doesn't see me.
I hide behind another *bare* tree.
Couldn't *bear* to have big *bear*
scare me, you see.
He moves his head from side to side,
then rolls on the ground and
roars the place down.
I'm ready to run from the big, brown *bear*
- make a sound of any kind I will not dare -
when out from behind the very *bare* tree,
appears a tiny figure that surprises me:
a cute, baby *bear* who me doesn't scare,
jumping up and down without a care.
He huddles beside the big, brown *bear*
who I now imagine is Daddy *bear*.
They play and play by the very *bare* tree
and not even once have they noticed me.

Bear, Bare

Explanation of each word:

Bear = a noun meaning a mammal having strong claws, a large head and a long coat.
Example: Watch out! There's a *bear* behind you!
Bear = a verb meaning to tolerate, endure or suffer.
Example: I cannot *bear* the pain.

Bare = an adjective meaning without a covering.
Example: The tree in the corner is very *bare*.

(**Bare** = an adjective meaning without suitable furnishings.
Example: Your bedroom is quite *bare*.)

Exercise 1

Oral activity

1) Listen to your teacher reading the poem aloud. What do you notice about your teacher's tone of voice? What kinds of gestures and facial expressions is your teacher using?
2) Practise reading the poem aloud. Listen to each reader's tone of voice. Look at the readers' gestures and facial expressions. Are they the same or different?
3) Discuss your reaction to the poem with your teacher and class. What do you like about the poem?

Exercise 2

Oral activity

Questions on the poem:

1) Why didn't the big bear see the poet?
2) What did the poet see the big bear doing from behind the bare tree?
3) What happened as the poet was about to run from the big bear?
4) What word in the poem is a synonym of *curls up* and *snuggles*?
5) *Rub* is a synonym of what word in the poem?

<u>*Exercise 3*</u>
Reading and Writing activity

Find the mistakes and rewrite each sentence correctly:

a) I'm not afraid of that big, ugly bare.

_____

_____

b) You can tell that it's winter because all the trees are bear.

_____

_____

c) They couldn't bare to lose another game.

_____

_____

d) Julia cannot find her new teddy bare.

_____

_____

<u>*Exercise 4*</u>
Reading and Writing activity

Match the following so that each sentence makes sense:

a) A baby bear   to look at it.
b) She can't bear   is called a cub.
c) The trees were   bare after the storm.
d) We saw a huge   bare after we cleared it out.
e) Our kitchen was quite   bear in the jungle.

Exercise 5

Writing activity

Write your own sentences and include *bear* in the first one, *bare* in the second one and both *bear* and *bare* in the last one:

1. (bear)

_____

_____

2. (bare)

_____

_____

3. (bear, bare)

_____

_____

<u>*Exercise 6*</u>

Writing and Reading activity

1) Write your own poem using either:
a) the word *bear* or *bare*

or

b) both words *bear* and *bare*

_____

_____

_____

_____

_____

_____

_____

_____

_____

_____

2) Read and recite your poem to your partner and then to your class.

3) Pick one poem you have listened to and discuss your favourite moment in it. Tell about an exciting character in the poem. Write what you liked about the poem.

_____

_____

_____

_____

_____

_____

_____

_____

_____

_____

_____

Blue, Blew

Teachers Notes

Before the lesson

The teacher should have a list of examples and demonstrate how we use gesture, tone of voice and facial expressions in our everyday lives.

The lesson

1) Write the words *blue* and *blew* on the whiteboard and elicit knowledge from pupils of each word. Looking at exercise 1, explain to pupils that they are going to listen to you reading aloud a poem called *Blue, Blew* and try to recall from the poem the difference in meaning and spelling between each word.

2) Refer pupils to the *Explanation of each word* section at the top of the first activity page for further explanation and examples. Invite pupils to give their own examples.

3) Discuss with the pupils common gestures, tones of voice and facial expressions that we use.

4) Pupils listen to you reading the poem aloud a second time and then discuss your tone of voice, gestures and facial expressions.

5) Individually or in pairs, pupils practise reading the poem aloud and note each reader's tone of voice, gestures and facial expressions.

6) Pupils discuss their reaction to the poem.

7) Ask pupils to answer orally, questions 1-5 on the poem (to check recall) without referring to the poem. (exercise 2)

8) Individually or in pairs, pupils complete true or false exercise. (no.3)

9) Individually or in pairs, pupils unscramble sentences containing each homophone learned. (exercise 4)

10) Pupils write their own sentences including each homophone. (exercise 5)

11) Pupils write their own poem using either one or both homophones (exercise 6 with b) being more challenging!). The poem should be at least 4 lines in length and does not have to rhyme. Invite pupils to read and recite their poem. Pupils then pick one poem they have listened to and write about their favourite moment in it, an exciting character and what they liked about the poem.

Any of the above exercises 3-6 could be given as homework exercises.

Answers

4) – 6) Teacher check

7) Exercise 2: 1) It blew away one windy afternoon. 2) It left him feeling blue. 3) Teacher check. 4) Teacher check. 5) blue

8) Exercise 3: 1) false; 2) true; 3) true; 4) false.

9) Exercise 4: 1) Our neighbour's garage door is painted blue and white. 2) The wind was so strong it blew ten slates off our roof. 3) My blue cap blew away one windy day.

10) Exercise 5: Teacher check

11) Exercise 6: Teacher check

Pupils could display their poems on the classroom wall(s).

Blue, Blew

Bobby had a *blue* balloon

that *blew* away one windy afternoon.

It *blew* so high

into the bright, *blue* sky.

No-one could catch it, not a single passer-by

- if only Bobby knew how to fly.

After it disappeared,

it left poor Bobby feeling *blue*.

That *blue* balloon that brought him

so much fun until one windy day, it *blew* away.

Where could it be? In a river or up a tree?

What was poor Bobby now to do?

Colour me blue.

Blue, Blew

Explanation of each word:

Blue = an adjective meaning of the colour blue.
Example: They dived into the deep, *blue* sea.
Blue = an adjective meaning sad, unhappy.
Example: She was feeling very *blue* because her puppy was missing.

Blew = the past tense of the verb *blow*.
Example: My ticket *blew* out of my hand.

Exercise 1

Oral activity

1) Listen to your teacher reading the poem aloud.
What do you notice about your teacher's tone of voice?
What kinds of gestures and facial expressions is your teacher using?
2) Practise reading the poem aloud. Listen to each reader's tone of voice.
Look at the readers' gestures and facial expressions.
Are they the same or different?
3) Discuss your reaction to the poem with your teacher and class.
What do you like about the poem?

Exercise 2

Oral activity

Questions on the poem:

1) What happened to Bobby's blue balloon?
2) How did Bobby feel about that?
3) What kind of fun do you think Bobby had with his balloon?
4) What could Bobby do now to have fun?
5) *Sad* and *unhappy* are synonyms of what word in the poem?

Exercise 3
Reading and Writing activity

True or False:
1) May I borrow your blew pen, please?_____
2) We have a new blue car._____
3) The strong wind blew my hat off._____
4) Tracy felt very blew when she discovered her dog was missing._____

Colour me blue.

Exercise 4
Writing activity

Can you unscramble the following sentences? (Remember to use a capital letter and full stop or question mark!):

1. garage is blue our and painted neighbour's door white

_____

_____

2. so the strong it wind slates was blew our off ten roof

_____

_____

3. away day my blew blue cap windy one

_____

_____

Exercise 5
Writing activity

Write your own sentences and include *blue* in the first one, *blew* in the second one and *blue* and *blew* in the last one:

1. (blue)

_____

_____

2. (blew)

_____

_____

3. (blue, blew)

_____

_____

<u>Exercise 6</u>

Writing and Reading activity

1) Write your own poem using either:
a) the word *blue* or *blew*
or
b) both words *blue* and *blew*

_____

_____

_____

_____

_____

_____

_____

_____

_____

_____

2) Read and recite your poem to your partner and then to your class.

3) Pick one poem you have listened to and discuss your favourite moment in it. Tell about an exciting character in the poem. Write what you liked about the poem.

_____

_____

_____

_____

_____

_____

_____

_____

_____

_____

_____

Breath, Breadth

Teachers Notes

Before the lesson

The teacher should have a list of examples and demonstrate how we use gesture, tone of voice and facial expressions in our everyday lives.

The lesson

1) Write the words *breath* and *breadth* on the whiteboard and elicit knowledge from pupils of each word. Looking at exercise 1, explain to pupils that they are going to listen to you reading aloud a poem called *Breath, Breadth* and try to recall from the poem the difference in meaning and spelling between each word.

2) Refer pupils to the *Explanation of each word* section at the top of the first activity page for further explanation and examples. Invite pupils to give their own examples.

3) Discuss with the pupils common gestures, tones of voice and facial expressions that we use.

4) Pupils listen to you reading the poem aloud a second time and then discuss your tone of voice, gestures and facial expressions.

5) Individually or in pairs, pupils practise reading the poem aloud and note each reader's tone of voice, gestures and facial expressions.

6) Pupils discuss their reaction to the poem.

7) Individually or in pairs, pupils match sentences containing each homophone learned. (exercise 2)

8) Individually or in pairs, pupils complete true or false exercise. (no.3)

9) Individually or in pairs, pupils complete find the mistakes exercise. (no.4)

10) Pupils write their own sentences including each homophone. (exercise 5)

11) Pupils write their own poem using either one or both homophones (exercise 6 with b) being more challenging!). The poem should be at least 4 lines in length and does not have to rhyme. Invite pupils to read and recite their poem. Pupils then pick one poem they have listened to and write about their favourite moment in it, an exciting character and what they liked about the poem.

Any of the above exercises 2 – 6 could be given as homework exercises.

Answers

4) – 6) Teacher check

7) Exercise 2: a) The beautiful sight took her breath away. b) Estimate the breadth of this table. c) He nearly lost his breath. d) My coach told me to take a deep breath. e) We searched the length and breadth of the room for it.

8) Exercise 3: 1) false; 2) true; 3) true; 4) false.

9) Exercise 4: a) They could hear every breath he took. b) It's rude to speak under your breath. c) We forgot to measure the breadth of the classroom. d) Take one breath slowly and deeply.

10) Exercise 5: Teacher check

11) Exercise 6: Teacher check

Pupils could display their poems on the classroom wall(s).

Breath, Breadth

As they travelled
the length and *breadth*
of this emerald isle,
its beauty took
their *breath* away
every single mile.

Before they swam
the *breadth* of the Liffey,
they drew a deep *breath*,
then jumped in
in a jiffy.

'How do I measure
the *breadth* of
my bedroom?'
Johnny muttered
under his *breath*.
'With your feet or
a metre stick,'
replied his friend Beth.

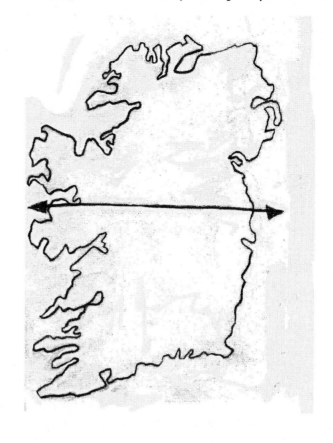

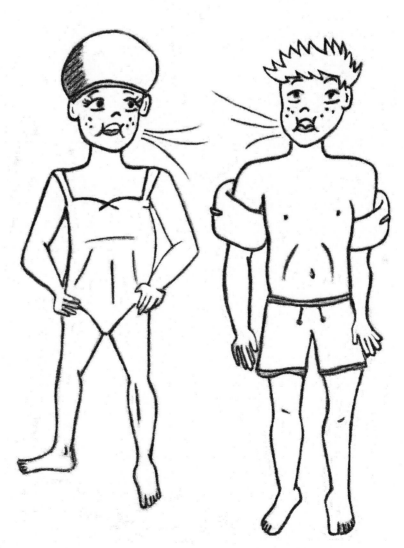

21

Breath, Breadth

Explanation of each word:

Breath = a noun meaning air which is inhaled or exhaled during breathing.
Example: Take a deep *breath*.

Breadth = a noun meaning the width of an object.
Example: Measure the *breadth* of your schoolyard.

Exercise 1

Oral activity

1) Listen to your teacher reading the poem aloud. What do you notice about your teacher's tone of voice? What kinds of gestures and facial expressions is your teacher using?
2) Practise reading the poem aloud. Listen to each reader's tone of voice. Look at the readers' gestures and facial expressions. Are they the same or different?
3) Discuss your reaction to the poem with your teacher and class. What do you like about the poem?

Exercise 2

Reading and Writing activity

Match the following so that each sentence makes sense:

a) The beautiful sight   of this table.
b) Estimate the breadth   to take a deep breath.
c) He nearly lost   and breadth of the room for it.
d) My coach told me   took her breath away.
e) We searched the length   his breath.

Exercise 3
Reading and Writing activity

True or False:
1) I could hardly catch my breadth._____
2) They swam the breadth of the lake._____
3) The picture takes his breath away every time he sees it._____
4) Did you work out the breath of your kitchen in centimetres?_____

Exercise 4
Reading and Writing activity

Find the mistakes and rewrite each sentence correctly:

a) They could hear every breadth he took.

_____

_____

b) It's rude to speak under your breadth.

_____

_____

c) We forgot to measure the breath of the classroom.

_____

_____

d) Take one breadth slowly and deeply.

_____

_____

Exercise 5
Writing activity

Write your own sentences and include *breath* in the first one, *breadth* in the second one and both *breath* and *breadth* in the last one:

1. (breath)

_____

_____

2. (breadth)

_____

_____

3. (breath, breadth)

_____

_____

Exercise 6

Writing and Reading activity

1) Write your own poem using either:
a) the word *breath* or *breadth*

or

b) both words *breath* and *breadth*

_____
_____
_____
_____
_____
_____
_____
_____
_____
_____

2) Read and recite your poem to your partner and then to your class.

3) Pick one poem you have listened to and discuss your favourite moment in it. Tell about an exciting character in the poem. Write what you liked about the poem.

_____
_____
_____
_____
_____
_____
_____
_____
_____
_____
_____

By, Bye, Buy

Teachers Notes

Before the lesson

The teacher should have a list of examples and demonstrate how we use gesture, tone of voice and facial expressions in our everyday lives.

The lesson

1) Write the words *by, bye* and *buy* on the whiteboard and elicit knowledge from pupils of each word. Looking at exercise 1, explain to pupils that they are going to listen to you reading aloud a poem called *By, Bye, Buy* and try to recall from the poem the difference in meaning and spelling between each word.

2) Refer pupils to the *Explanation of each word* section at the top of the first activity page for further explanation and examples. Invite pupils to give their own examples.

3) Discuss with the pupils common gestures, tones of voice and facial expressions that we use.

4) Pupils listen to you reading the poem aloud a second time and then discuss your tone of voice, gestures and facial expressions.

5) Individually or in pairs, pupils practise reading the poem aloud and note each reader's tone of voice, gestures and facial expressions.

6) Pupils discuss their reaction to the poem.

7) Ask pupils to answer orally, questions 1-5 on the poem (to check recall) without referring to the poem. (exercise 2)

8) Individually or in pairs, pupils complete true or false exercise. (no.3)

9) Individually or in pairs, pupils unscramble sentences containing each of the homophones learned. (exercise 4)

10) Pupils write their own sentences including each homophone. (exercise 5)

11) Pupils write their own poem using either one, two or all three homophones (exercise 6 with b) and c) being more challenging!). The poem should be at least 4 lines in length and does not have to rhyme. Invite pupils to read and recite their poem. Pupils then pick one poem they have listened to and write about their favourite moment in it, an exciting character and what they liked about the poem.

Any of the above exercises 3 – 6 could be given as homework exercises.

Answers

4) – 6) Teacher check

7) Exercise 2: 1) to buy some bread; 2) Greg the Grocer and Harry; 3) he was off to buy some pie; 4) get/purchase/pay for/obtain; 5) hi/hello/good day

8) Exercise 3: 1) false; 2) false; 3) true; 4) false; 5) true

9) Exercise 4: 1) They bought an ice-cream and sat by a tree. 2) He would like his Mum to buy him a new bicycle for his birthday. 3) The children chatted together and then they waved each other goodbye.

10) Exercise 5: Teacher check

11) Exercise 6: Teacher check

Pupils could display their poems on the classroom wall(s).

By, Bye, Buy

On Bob's way into town
to *buy* some bread,
he passed *by* a house
painted white and red.

Right *by* the front door,
he saw Greg the Grocer
talking to Harry from
the new hardware store.

Pointing to the sky,
Greg raised his head high
and watched a loud
aeroplane flying *by*.

He took a few steps back,
and held his hand high.
He said to Harry: 'I'm off to *buy* some pie!'
and then waved him good*bye*.

27

By, Bye, Buy

Explanation of each word:

By = a preposition meaning passing the position of or past.
Example: We walked *by* the old mill.
By = a preposition meaning next to, near or beside.
Example: He is at the bus stop *by* the shop.

Bye = an informal word for *goodbye*.
Example: '*Bye* now,' said Mary.

Buy = a verb meaning to get something by paying money, to purchase.
Example: Make sure you *buy* yourself some sweets.

Exercise 1
Oral activity

1) Listen to your teacher reading the poem aloud. What do you notice about your teacher's tone of voice? What kinds of gestures and facial expressions is your teacher using?
2) Practise reading the poem aloud. Listen to each reader's tone of voice. Look at the readers' gestures and facial expressions. Are they the same or different?
3) Discuss your reaction to the poem with your teacher and class. What do you like about the poem?

Exercise 2
Oral activity

Questions on the poem:
1) Why was Bob going into town?
2) Who did Bob see right by the front door of the house?
3) What did Greg say to Harry?
4) What synonyms do you know of the word *buy*?
5) What antonyms do you know of the word *bye*?

Exercise 3
Reading and Writing activity

True or False:
1) If you want to by a new dress, you'll have to save some money. _____
2) Mark said by to Joe and then hung up. _____
3) I need to buy some more paint. _____
4) We went on a nature walk down bye the river. _____
5) They passed by a football stadium on their way into town. _____

Exercise 4
Writing activity

Can you unscramble the following sentences? (Remember to use a capital letter and full stop or question mark!):

1. by sat they tree bought and ice-cream an a

_____

_____

2. like for to he would buy bicycle Mum his him new a birthday his

_____

_____

3. chatted goodbye then children and the each other together they waved

_____

_____

Exercise 5

Writing activity

Write your own sentences and include *by* in the first one, *bye* in the second one and *buy* in the last one:

1. (by)

_____

_____

2. (bye)

_____

_____

3. (buy)

_____

_____

<u>*Exercise 6*</u>

Writing and Reading activity

1) Write your own poem using either:
a) the word *by*, *bye*, or *buy*
> or
b) the words *by* and *bye* or *by* and *buy*
> or
c) all three words *by*, *bye* and *buy*

_____
_____
_____
_____
_____
_____
_____
_____
_____
_____

2) Read and recite your poem to your partner and then to your class.

3) Pick one poem you have listened to and discuss your favourite moment in it. Tell about an exciting character in the poem. Write what you liked about the poem.

_____
_____
_____
_____
_____
_____
_____
_____
_____
_____

Flower, Flour

Teachers Notes

Before the lesson

The teacher should have a list of examples and demonstrate how we use gesture, tone of voice and facial expressions in our everyday lives.

The lesson

1) Write the words *flower* and *flour* on the whiteboard and elicit knowledge from pupils of each word. Looking at exercise 1, explain to pupils that they are going to listen to you reading aloud a poem called *Flower, Flour* and try to recall from the poem the difference in meaning and spelling between each word.

2) Refer pupils to the *Explanation of each word* section at the top of the first activity page for further explanation and examples. Invite pupils to give their own examples.

3) Discuss with the pupils common gestures, tones of voice and facial expressions that we use.

4) Pupils listen to you reading the poem aloud a second time and then discuss your tone of voice, gestures and facial expressions.

5) Individually or in pairs, pupils practise reading the poem aloud and note each reader's tone of voice, gestures and facial expressions.

6) Pupils discuss their reaction to the poem.

7) Individually or in pairs, pupils complete fill in the blanks exercise. (no.2)

8) Pupils find both homophones in the wordsearch. The words are written either backwards, diagonally, vertically or horizontally. (exercise 3)

9) Individually or in pairs, pupils complete true or false exercise. (no.4)

10) Pupils write their own sentences including each homophone. (exercise 5)

11) Pupils write their own poem using either one or both homophones (exercise 6 with b) being more challenging!). The poem should be at least 4 lines in length and does not have to rhyme. Invite pupils to read and recite their poem. Pupils then pick one poem they have listened to and write about their favourite moment in it, an exciting character and what they liked about the poem.

Any of the above exercises 2 – 6 could be given as homework exercises.

Answers

4) – 6) Teacher check

7) Exercise 2: a) flour; b) flower; c) flower; d) flour; e) flour; f) flower

8) Exercise 3:

m	*f*	s	r	*f*	*f*	e
i	a	*l*	e	*l*	o	g
n	e	q	*o*	*o*	w	v
c	b	*w*	q	*u*	h	u
u	*e*	f	l	*r*	*r*	s
r	*r*	*e*	*w*	*o*	*l*	f
p	s	i	f	l	r	o

9) Exercise 4: 1) true; 2) false; 3) true; 4) false.

10) Exercise 5: Teacher check

11) Exercise 6: Teacher check

Pupils could display their poems on the classroom wall(s).

Flower, Flour

A *f l o w e r* is a scented blossom
that grows in your garden.
It has a green stem and petals
and likes lots of water.

Flowers come in all sorts of colours.
You'll see them in pretty pictures,
on patterns in carpets,
clothes and duvet covers.

F l o u r is that fine, white powder
we use in baking.
Cakes, buns, breads,
ruff puff pastry -
what are you making?

F l o u r can be sprinkled
over a freshly baked treat
for a snowy effect
or to add some colour,
just before it's ready to eat.

Flower, Flour

Explanation of each word:

Flower = a noun meaning a blossom that grows in a garden.
Example: He gave her a very pretty *flower*.

Flour = a noun meaning a fine or coarse powder made from wheat.
Example: Add half the *flour* to the mixture.

Exercise 1
Oral activity

1) Listen to your teacher reading the poem aloud. What do you notice about your teacher's tone of voice? What kinds of gestures and facial expressions is your teacher using?
2) Practise reading the poem aloud. Listen to each reader's tone of voice. Look at the readers' gestures and facial expressions. Are they the same or different?
3) Discuss your reaction to the poem with your teacher and class. What do you like about the poem?

Exercise 2
Reading and Writing activity

Read the poem and then see if you can fill in the blanks using *flower* or *flour*:
a) Add the _____ and sugar to the mixing bowl.
b) The daffodil is my favourite _____.
c) Judy went into the garden and picked a pretty _____.
d) Sprinkle with _____ and then it's ready to serve.
e) Use plenty of _____ when making these scones.
f) A withered _____ lay on the ground.

Exercise 3

Writing activity

The words *flower* and *flour* appear twice in the wordsearch below. Can you find them?

Write the words here:

1)_____
2)_____
3)_____
4)_____

m	f	s	r	f	f	e
i	a	l	e	l	o	g
n	e	q	o	o	w	v
c	b	w	q	u	h	u
u	e	f	l	r	r	s
r	r	e	w	o	l	f
p	s	i	f	l	r	o

Exercise 4

Reading and Writing activity

True or False:
1) How much flour do I need to add?_____
2) Can you count the petals on this flour?_____
3) This is a very sweet-scented flower._____
4) Which flower is better? Cream or self-raising?_____

Exercise 5

Writing activity

Write your own sentences and include *flower* in the first one and *flour* in the second one.

1. (flower)

_____

_____

2. (flour)

_____

_____

Exercise 6

Writing and Reading activity

1) Write your own poem using either:
a) the word *flower* or *flour*

or

b) both words *flower* and *flour*

_____

_____

_____

_____

_____

_____

_____

_____

_____

_____

2) Read and recite your poem to your partner and then to your class.

3) Pick one poem you have listened to and discuss your favourite moment in it. Tell about an exciting character in the poem. Write what you liked about the poem.

_____

_____

_____

_____

_____

_____

_____

_____

_____

_____

_____

Hair, Hare

Teachers Notes

Before the lesson

The teacher should have a list of examples and demonstrate how we use gesture, tone of voice and facial expressions in our everyday lives.

The lesson

1) Write the words *hair* and *hare* on the whiteboard and elicit knowledge from pupils of each word. Looking at exercise 1, explain to pupils that they are going to listen to you reading aloud a poem called *Hair, Hare* and try to recall from the poem the difference in meaning and spelling between each word.
2) Refer pupils to the *Explanation of each word* section at the top of the first activity page for further explanation and examples. Invite pupils to give their own examples.
3) Discuss with the pupils common gestures, tones of voice and facial expressions that we use.
4) Pupils listen to you reading the poem aloud a second time and then discuss your tone of voice, gestures and facial expressions.
5) Individually or in pairs, pupils practise reading the poem aloud and note each reader's tone of voice, gestures and facial expressions.
6) Pupils discuss their reaction to the poem.
7) Ask pupils to answer orally, questions 1-5 on the poem (to check recall) without referring to the poem. (exercise 2)
8) Individually or in pairs, pupils unscramble sentences containing both homophones learned. (exercise 3)
9) Individually or in pairs, pupils complete fill in the blanks exercise. (no.4)
10) Pupils write their own sentences including each homophone. (exercise 5)
11) Pupils write their own poem using either one or both homophones (exercise 6 with b) being more challenging!). The poem should be at least 4 lines in length and does not have to rhyme. Invite pupils to read and recite their poem. Pupils then pick one poem they have listened to and write about their favourite moment in it, an exciting character and what they liked about the poem.

Any of the above exercises 3-6 could be given as homework exercises.

Answers

4) – 6) Teacher check
7) Exercise 2: 1) a March hare; 2) in a shallow nest; 3) Teacher check; 4) Teacher check; 5) over/above
8) Exercise 3: 1) I must go and get my hair cut on Saturday. 2) I have never seen anything run faster than a hare. 3) Do you know the difference between the words <u>hare</u> and <u>hair</u>?
9) Exercise 4: a) hair; b) hair; c) hare; d) hair; e) hare; f) hair
10) Exercise 5: Teacher check
11) Exercise 6: Teacher check

Pupils could display their poems on the classroom wall(s).

Hair, Hare

Oh where oh where
would I see a March *hare*?
I've never seen one before,
I swear, I swear.
What colour is its fur
or is it *hair*?
Black, brown, white or fair?
How would I know a
rabbit from a *hare*?
Are its legs a lot shorter
and does it have less fur
or should I say *hair*?
Does a *hare* live in a burrow
or a nest beneath a tree?
Might I see one in Mum's garden
nibbling her lettuce leaves for tea?

Hair, Hare

Explanation of each word:

Hair = a noun meaning threadlike structures that grow from follicles beneath the skin.
Example: He has short, curly *hair*.

Hare = a noun meaning a mammal which is larger than a rabbit.
Example: The dog ran after the *hare*.

Exercise 1
Oral activity

1) Listen to your teacher reading the poem aloud. What do you notice about your teacher's tone of voice? What kinds of gestures and facial expressions is your teacher using?
2) Practise reading the poem aloud. Listen to each reader's tone of voice. Look at the readers' gestures and facial expressions. Are they the same or different?
3) Discuss your reaction to the poem with your teacher and class. What do you like about the poem?

Exercise 2
Oral activity

Questions on the poem:
1) What has the poet never seen before?
2) The poet doesn't know where a hare lives. Do you know?
3) Where do you think you would see a hare?
4) Have you ever seen a hare? If so, mention where you saw it and describe it.
5) What is the antonym of the word *beneath* in the poem?

Exercise 3

Writing activity

Can you unscramble the following sentences? (Remember to use a capital letter and full stop or question mark!)

1. go hair I Saturday get must and cut my on

_____

_____

2. seen than have hare I run never a faster anything

_____

_____

3. between you hair difference do and the hare know words the

_____

_____

Exercise 4

Reading and Writing activity

Read the poem and then see if you can fill in the blanks using *hair* or *hare*:
a) Katie has very long black _____.
b) Her grandmother used to comb her _____ every morning.
c) Just look at how fast that _____ can run.
d) All the boys had short, brown _____.
e) The _____ cocked up its ears and then darted into the ditch.
f) Did you see Jane's new _____style?

Exercise 5
Writing activity

Write your own sentences and include *hair* in the first one, *hare* in the second one and both *hair* and *hare* in the last one:

1. (hair)

_____

_____

2. (hare)

_____

_____

3. (hair, hare)

_____

_____

Exercise 6
Writing and Reading activity

1) Write your own poem using either:
a) the word *hair* or *hare*
                        or
b) both words *hair* and *hare*

_____

_____

_____

_____

_____

_____

_____

_____

2) Read and recite your poem to your partner and then to your class.

3) Pick one poem you have listened to and discuss your favourite moment in it. Tell about an exciting character in the poem. Write what you liked about the poem.

_____

_____

_____

_____

_____

_____

_____

_____

_____

_____

_____

Herd, Heard

Teachers Notes

Before the lesson

The teacher should have a list of examples and demonstrate how we use gesture, tone of voice and facial expressions in our everyday lives.

The lesson

1) Write the words *herd* and *heard* on the whiteboard and elicit knowledge from pupils of each word. Looking at exercise 1, explain to pupils that they are going to listen to you reading aloud a poem called *Herd, Heard* and try to recall from the poem the difference in meaning and spelling between each word.

2) Refer pupils to the *Explanation of each word* section at the top of the first activity page for further explanation and examples. Invite pupils to give their own examples.

3) Discuss with the pupils common gestures, tones of voice and facial expressions that we use.

4) Pupils listen to you reading the poem aloud a second time and then discuss your tone of voice, gestures and facial expressions.

5) Individually or in pairs, pupils practise reading the poem aloud and note each reader's tone of voice, gestures and facial expressions.

6) Pupils discuss their reaction to the poem.

7) Ask pupils to answer orally, questions 1-5 on the poem (to check recall) without referring to the poem. (exercise 2)

8) Individually or in pairs, pupils complete find the mistakes exercise. (no.3)

9) Individually or in pairs, pupils complete fill in the blanks exercise. (no.4)

10) Individually or in pairs, pupils match sentences containing each homophone learned (exercise 5).

11) Pupils write their own poem using either one or both homophones (exercise 6 with b) being more challenging!). The poem should be at least 4 lines in length and does not have to rhyme. Invite pupils to read and recite their poem. Pupils then pick one poem they have listened to and write about their favourite moment in it, an exciting character and what they liked about the poem.

Any of the above exercises 3 – 6 could be given as homework exercises.

Answers

4) – 6) Teacher check

7) Exercise 2: 1) an almighty stampede; 2) on Saturday morning; 3) her roses; 4) screaming; 5) fuss

8) Exercise 3: a) Luke saw a herd of buffaloes on holiday. b) We heard a herd of heifers jumping over a high wall. c) I never heard a herd run so fast. d) Tara said that she heard a loud bang in the garden.

9) Exercise 4: a) heard; b) herd; c) heard; d) heard; e) herd; f) heard

10) Exercise 5: a) I think I heard a noise back there. b) The herd was seen running all over the lawn. c) We never heard you coming *or* We never heard you whistling in the kitchen. d) I heard your father bought a new herd of cattle. e) They heard the baby crying next door. f) She thought she heard you coming *or* She thought she heard you whistling in the kitchen.

11) Exercise 6: Teacher check

Pupils could display their poems on the classroom wall(s).

Herd, Heard

I *heard* an almighty stampede
as I looked out my window
on Saturday morning.
A big *herd* of cows
running all over the lawn
without any warning.

Where did this *herd* come from?
How will we stop them running about?
'My flowers, my flowers!'
I *heard* Mum screaming out.

Dad to the rescue
to hurl the *herd* out
and save Mum's roses
from being pulled out.
A neighbour was *heard* later
asking what all the fuss was about:
a break-in to a garden
by a big *herd*, which broke out!

Herd, Heard

Explanation of each word:

Herd = a noun meaning a large group of mammals.
Example: The farmer has a big *herd* of cattle.
Herd = a verb meaning to look after (mammals).
Example: He is *herd*ing his sheep.

Heard = the past tense of the verb *hear*.
Example: I *heard* you calling for Rosie.

Exercise 1
Oral activity

1) Listen to your teacher reading the poem aloud. What do you notice about your teacher's tone of voice? What kinds of gestures and facial expressions is your teacher using?
2) Practise reading the poem aloud. Listen to each reader's tone of voice. Look at the readers' gestures and facial expressions. Are they the same or different?
3) Discuss your reaction to the poem with your teacher and class. What do you like about the poem?

Exercise 2
Oral activity

Questions on the poem:
1) What did the poet hear as she looked out her window?
2) When did she hear it?
3) Which of Mum's flowers did Dad save?
4) What word in the poem is a synonym of *yelling*?
5) *Upset* and *worry* are synonyms of what word in the poem?

Exercise 3
Reading and Writing activity

Find the mistakes and rewrite each sentence correctly:
a) Luke saw a heard of buffaloes on holiday.

_____

_____

b) We herd a herd of heifers jumping over a high wall.

_____

_____

c) I never herd a heard run so fast.

_____

_____

d) Tara said that she herd a loud bang in the garden.

_____

_____

Exercise 4
Reading and Writing activity

Read the poem and then see if you can fill in the blanks using *herd* or *heard*:
a) We _____ a beautiful piece of music.
b) The farmer could not find his _____.
c) Lucy _____ that it was snowing in the midlands.
d) I _____ nothing in the room.
e) Dad is going to the mart to buy a new _____.
f) They never _____ anything like it before.

Exercise 5

Reading and Writing activity

Match the following so that each sentence makes sense:

a) I think I heard   heard you coming.
b) The herd was seen   bought a new herd of cattle.
c) We never   baby crying next door.
d) I heard your father   running all over the lawn.
e) They heard the   heard you whistling in the kitchen.
f) She thought she   a noise back there.

Exercise 6

Writing and Reading activity

1) Write your own poem using either:
a) the word *herd* or *heard*

or

b) both words *herd* and *heard*

_____

_____

_____

_____

_____

_____

_____

_____

_____

2) Read and recite your poem to your partner and then to your class.

3) Pick one poem you have listened to and discuss your favourite moment in it. Tell about an exciting character in the poem. Write what you liked about the poem.

_____

_____

_____

_____

_____

_____

_____

_____

_____

_____

_____

Here, Hear

Teachers Notes

Before the lesson

The teacher should have a list of examples and demonstrate how we use gesture, tone of voice and facial expressions in our everyday lives.

The lesson

1) Write the words *here* and *hear* on the whiteboard and elicit knowledge from pupils of each word. Looking at exercise 1, explain to pupils that they are going to listen to you reading aloud a poem called *Here, Hear* and try to recall from the poem the difference in meaning and spelling between each word.
2) Refer pupils to the *Explanation of each word* section at the top of the first activity page for further explanation and examples. Invite pupils to give their own examples.
3) Discuss with the pupils common gestures, tones of voice and facial expressions that we use.
4) Pupils listen to you reading the poem aloud a second time and then discuss your tone of voice, gestures and facial expressions.
5) Individually or in pairs, pupils practise reading the poem aloud and note each reader's tone of voice, gestures and facial expressions.
6) Pupils discuss their reaction to the poem.
7) Ask pupils to answer orally, questions 1-5 on the poem (to check recall) without referring to the poem. (exercise 2)
8) Individually or in pairs, pupils match sentences containing each homophone learned.(exercise 3)
9) Pupils write their own sentences including each homophone. (exercise 4)
10) Individually or in pairs, pupils complete fill in the blanks exercise. (no. 5)
11) Pupils write their own poem using either one or both homophones (exercise 6 with b) being more challenging!). The poem should be at least 4 lines in length and does not have to rhyme. Invite pupils to read and recite their poem. Pupils then pick one poem they have listened to and write about their favourite moment in it, an exciting character and what they liked about the poem.

Any of the above exercises 3 – 6 could be given as homework exercises

Answers

4) – 6) Teacher check
7) Exercise 2: 1) her guitar case; 2) washing the dishes; 3) Ben; 4) in the attic *or* a room upstairs; 5) unfair
8) Exercise 3: a) She cannot hear you very well. b) Put the box down right here. c) I can hear a lot of noise outside. d) Here is the book you were looking for. e) There are too many cooks in here.
9) Exercise 4: Teacher check
10) Exercise 5: a) hear; b) here; c) hear, here; d) here; e) hear; f) here.
11) Exercise 6: Teacher check

Pupils could display their poems on the classroom wall(s).

Here, Hear

It's so quiet in *here*,
I cannot *hear* a sound.
I'm looking for my
guitar case
and it's nowhere
to be found.
I *hear* Mum
in the kitchen
washing the dishes
and in need of some help.
I know it's unfair
but I'm glad to be up *here*
and not down there.
Searching and searching,
I don't think it's *here*.
If only I could remember
where I left it last year!
I *hear* Ben and Jen
laughing out loud.
Will I ask them up *here*
to help me out?
'*Here* it is!' I *hear* Ben shout.
Found it at last -
my brown, dusty case.
Right *here* by my feet
I'll make some space
and create for it
its own special place.

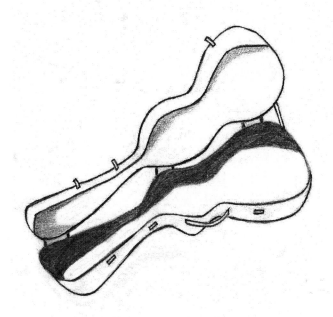

Here, Hear

Explanation of each word:

Here = an adverb meaning in, at or to this place.
Example: Come over *here* for one minute.

Hear = a verb meaning to listen to.
Example: Did you *hear* my good news?

Exercise 1
Oral activity

1) Listen to your teacher reading the poem aloud. What do you notice about your teacher's tone of voice? What kinds of gestures and facial expressions is your teacher using?
2) Practise reading the poem aloud. Listen to each reader's tone of voice. Look at the readers' gestures and facial expressions. Are they the same or different?
3) Discuss your reaction to the poem with your teacher and class. What do you like about the poem?

Exercise 2
Oral activity

Questions on the poem:

1) What is the poet looking for in the poem?
2) What is Mum doing in the kitchen?
3) Who finds what the poet is looking for?
4) Where do you think the poet is?
5) What word in the poem is a synonym of *unjust*?

Exercise 3
Reading and Writing activity

Match the following so that each sentence makes sense:

a) She cannot   a lot of noise outside.
b) Put the box   you were looking for.
c) I can hear   down right here.
d) Here is the book   hear you very well.
e) There are too many   cooks in here.

Exercise 4
Writing activity
Write your own sentences and include *here* in the first one, *hear* in the second one and both *here* and *hear* in the last one:

1. (here)

_____

_____

2. (hear)

_____

_____

3. (here, hear)

_____

_____

Exercise 5
Reading and Writing activity

Read the poem and then see if you can fill in the blanks using *here* or *hear*:

a) Did you _____ what happened to the postman?

b) There is nobody in _____.

c) I _____ the baby crying. Please take her up and bring her down _____.

d) She was standing right _____ beside me.

e) We _____ the same story every day.

f) It looks like the snow is _____ to stay.

Exercise 6
Writing and Reading activity

1) Write your own poem using either:

a) the word *here* or *hear*

                    or

b) both words *here* and *hear*

_____

_____

_____

_____

_____

_____

_____

_____

_____

2) Read and recite your poem to your partner and then to your class.

3) Pick one poem you have listened to and discuss your favourite moment in it. Tell about an exciting character in the poem. Write what you liked about the poem.

_____

_____

_____

_____

_____

_____

_____

_____

_____

_____

It's, Its

Teachers Notes

Before the lesson

The teacher should have a list of examples and demonstrate how we use gesture, tone of voice and facial expressions in our everyday lives.

The lesson

1) Write the words *it's* and *its* on the whiteboard and elicit knowledge from pupils of each word. Looking at exercise 1, explain to pupils that they are going to listen to you reading aloud a poem called *It's, Its* and try to recall from the poem the difference in meaning and spelling between each word.

2) Refer pupils to the *Explanation of each word* section at the top of the first activity page for further explanation and examples. Invite pupils to give their own examples.

3) Discuss with the pupils common gestures, tones of voice and facial expressions that we use.

4) Pupils listen to you reading the poem aloud a second time and then discuss your tone of voice, gestures and facial expressions.

5) Individually or in pairs, pupils practise reading the poem aloud and note each reader's tone of voice, gestures and facial expressions.

6) Pupils discuss their reaction to the poem.

7) Individually or in pairs, pupils complete fill in the blanks exercise. (no.2)

8) Individually or in pairs, pupils unscramble sentences containing each homophone learned (exercise 3).

9) Individually or in pairs, pupils complete find the mistakes exercise. (no.4)

10) Pupils write their own sentences including each homophone. (exercise 5)

11) Pupils write their own poem using either one or both homophones (exercise 6 with b) being more challenging!). The poem should be at least 4 lines in length and does not have to rhyme. Invite pupils to read and recite their poem. Pupils then pick one poem they have listened to and write about their favourite moment in it, an exciting character and what they liked about the poem.

Any of the above exercises 2 - 6 could be given as homework exercises.

Answers

4) – 6) Teacher check

7) Exercise 2: a) It's; b) its; c) It's; d) It's; e) It's; f) its.

8) Exercise 3: 1) It's so exciting to be travelling to the south of France. 2) It's a real pity that you couldn't come to my party. 3) What have you done to its wheel and window?

9) Exercise 4: a) I think it's a good time for us to make some cookies. b) It's just that I'm not that sure about its size and shape. c) If you look at its face, you'll see that it's got black spots and long whiskers.

10) Exercise 5: Teacher check

11) Exercise 6: Teacher check

Pupils could display their poems on the classroom wall(s).

It's, Its

It's not every day
that the sun comes out
and shines all day.

Its heat warms our bodies
when we're outside at play.
Its magical colour helps
brighten our mood in every way.

It's your wish and my wish
to have fun in the sun.
If only it would appear
for everyone.

Its rays beam down
and remove our frown.
It's a pity it stops shining
in this quiet, little town.

It's got to come out
and cheer us up.
Please, let it show *its* face
and scatter itself about
this dark, dreary place.

It's, Its

Explanation of each word:

It's = a contraction of the words *it is* or *it has*.
Example: *It's* a very wet day. *It's* got whiskers and a long tail.

Its = a possessive adjective meaning belonging to it or of it.
Example: I like *its* colour and flavour.

Exercise 1
Oral activity

1) Listen to your teacher reading the poem aloud. What do you notice about your teacher's tone of voice? What kinds of gestures and facial expressions is your teacher using?
2) Practise reading the poem aloud. Listen to each reader's tone of voice. Look at the readers' gestures and facial expressions. Are they the same or different?
3) Discuss your reaction to the poem with your teacher and class. What do you like about the poem?

Exercise 2
Reading and Writing activity

Read the poem and then see if you can fill in the blanks using *it's* or *its*:
a) _____ just what I wanted.
b) The little bird has hurt _____ wing.
c) _____ not every day you get to swim, play football and go horse-riding.
d) We have a new house. _____ got four big bedrooms and two bathrooms.
e) _____ great that you can come and stay.
f) Our garden tree has lost all of _____ leaves.

Exercise 3
Writing activity

Can you unscramble the following sentences? (Remember to use a capital letter and full stop or question mark!):

1. so travelling it's be to exciting to of the France south

_____

_____

2. pity come you that party couldn't my a it's real to

_____

_____

3. to you what its done have and wheel window

_____

_____

Exercise 4
Reading and Writing activity

Find the mistakes and rewrite each sentence correctly:
a) I think its a good time for us to make some cookies.

_____

_____

b) Its just that I'm not that sure about it's size and shape.

_____

_____

c) If you look at it's face, you'll see that its got black spots and long whiskers.

_____

_____

Exercise 5
Writing activity

Write your own sentences and include *its* in the first one, *it's* in the second one and both *its* and *it's* in the last one:

1. (its)

_____

_____

2. (it's)

_____

_____

3. (its, it's)

_____

_____

Exercise 6
Writing and Reading activity

1) Write your own poem using either:
a) the words *its* or *it's*
                    or
b) both words *its* and *it's*

_____

_____

_____

_____

_____

_____

_____

_____

_____

2) Read and recite your poem to your partner and then to your class.

3) Pick one poem you have listened to and discuss your favourite moment in it. Tell about an exciting character in the poem. Write what you liked about the poem.

_____

_____

_____

_____

_____

_____

_____

_____

_____

_____

_____

New, Knew

Teachers Notes

Before the lesson

The teacher should have a list of examples and demonstrate how we use gesture, tone of voice and facial expressions in our everyday lives.

The lesson

1) Write the words *new* and *knew* on the whiteboard and elicit knowledge from pupils of each word. Looking at exercise 1, explain to pupils that they are going to listen to you reading aloud a poem called *New, Knew* and try to recall from the poem the difference in meaning and spelling between each word.

2) Refer pupils to the *Explanation of each word* section at the top of the first activity page for further explanation and examples. Invite pupils to give their own examples.

3) Discuss with the pupils common gestures, tones of voice and facial expressions that we use.

4) Pupils listen to you reading the poem aloud a second time and then discuss your tone of voice, gestures and facial expressions.

5) Individually or in pairs, pupils practise reading the poem aloud and note each reader's tone of voice, gestures and facial expressions.

6) Pupils discuss their reaction to the poem.

7) Ask pupils to answer orally, questions 1-5 on the poem (to check recall) without referring to the poem. (exercise 2)

8) Individually or in pairs, pupils complete fill in the blanks exercise. (no.3)

9) Pupils write their own sentences including each homophone. (exercise 4)

10) Individually or in pairs, pupils complete find the mistakes exercise. (no.5)

11) Pupils write their own poem using either one or both homophones (exercise 6 with b) being more challenging!). The poem should be at least 4 lines in length and does not have to rhyme. Invite pupils to read and recite their poem. Pupils then pick one poem they have listened to and write about their favourite moment in it, an exciting character and what they liked about the poem.

Any of the above exercises 3 – 6 could be given as homework exercises.

Answers

4) – 6) Teacher check

7) Exercise 2: 1) a book; 2) Mum; 3) Jack the Lad; 4) a boat; 5) arrived back

8) Exercise 3: a) new; b) knew; c) knew; d) new; e) knew, new; f) knew, new

9) Exercise 4: Teacher check

10) Exercise 5: Correct homophone is on the last line "....to buy his *new* jersey."

11) Exercise 6: Teacher check

Pupils could display their poems on the classroom wall(s).

New, Knew

I *knew* that you were happy
when you got your *new* book.
You showed it to everyone
you *knew* at school and
invited them all to
take a good look.

Mum *knew* that your
brand *new* shoes
were a little too tight.
But that didn't matter-
their colour and design
were oh so right!

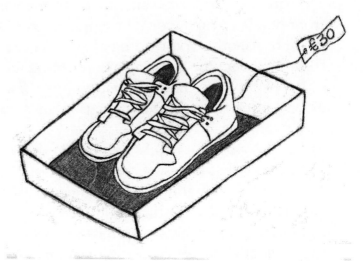

Your friends *knew* that
you were sad when
you lost your *new* puppy
named 'Jack the Lad'.
You searched and searched
with all your might
until he arrived back
on your doorstep
and gave you a fright!

Dad *knew* that you
weren't too pleased to wear
your brand *new* coat.
But at least it kept you warm
on his brand *new* boat.

New, Knew

Explanation of each word:

New = an adjective meaning recently made or brought into being.
Example: I need *new* shoes.

Knew = the past tense of the verb *know*.
Example: She *knew* that she was right.

Exercise 1
Oral activity

1) Listen to your teacher reading the poem aloud. What do you notice about your teacher's tone of voice? What kinds of gestures and facial expressions is your teacher using?
2) Practise reading the poem aloud. Listen to each reader's tone of voice. Look at the readers' gestures and facial expressions. Are they the same or different?
3) Discuss your reaction to the poem with your teacher and class. What do you like about the poem?

Exercise 2
Oral activity

Questions on the poem:

1) What new item does the poet mention in the first verse of the poem?
2) Who knew that the brand new shoes were a little too tight?
3) What was the name of the lost puppy?
4) What did Dad recently buy?
5) The word *returned* is a synonym of what two words in the poem?

Exercise 3
Reading and Writing activity
Read the poem and see if you can fill in the blanks using *new* or *knew*:
a) Mum bought John a _____ football for his birthday.
b) I wish I _____ what to do.
c) The children _____ their multiplication tables.
d) Tracy and Paul need a _____ copy.
e) Dad _____ that Sarah wanted a _____ book about animals.
f) He _____ that she was going to buy a _____ car.

Exercise 4

Writing activity

Write your own sentences and include *new* in the first one, *knew* in the second one and both *new* and *knew* in the last one:

1. (new)

_____

_____

2. (knew)

_____

_____

3. (new, knew)

_____

_____

Exercise 5

Reading and Writing activity

Find the mistakes and underline each one. Write the correct word over each incorrect word. (One is correct!)

Tim new what he had to do if he wanted to get a knew football jersey. He new he would have to help out at home with the daily chores. He started on Monday by washing the dishes and hoovering the sitting room. Mum new what Tim's plan was and gladly remarked how the sitting room carpet looked as good as knew. He cleaned out the garage and helped Dad assemble his brand knew shelf. Dad never new his son could be so tidy and helpful. Tim finished his chores on Friday and went into town on the knew 128 bus to buy his new jersey.

Exercise 6
Writing and Reading activity

1) Write your own poem using either:
a) the word *new* or *knew*
> or
b) both words *new* and *knew*

_____

_____

_____

_____

_____

_____

_____

_____

_____

_____

2) Read and recite your poem to your partner and then to your class.

3) Pick one poem you have listened to and discuss your favourite moment in it. Tell about an exciting character in the poem. Write what you liked about the poem.

_____

_____

_____

_____

_____

_____

_____

_____

_____

_____

_____

_____

No, Know

Teachers Notes

Before the lesson

The teacher should have a list of examples and demonstrate how we use gesture, tone of voice and facial expressions in our everyday lives.

The lesson

1) Write the words *no* and *know* on the whiteboard and elicit knowledge from pupils of each word. Looking at exercise 1, explain to pupils that they are going to listen to you reading aloud a poem called *No, Know* and try to recall from the poem the difference in meaning and spelling between each word.

2) Refer pupils to the *Explanation of each word* section at the top of the first activity page for further explanation and examples. Invite pupils to give their own examples.

3) Discuss with the pupils common gestures, tones of voice and facial expressions that we use.

4) Pupils listen to you reading the poem aloud a second time and then discuss your tone of voice, gestures and facial expressions.

5) Individually or in pairs, pupils practise reading the poem aloud and note each reader's tone of voice, gestures and facial expressions.

6) Pupils discuss their reaction to the poem.

7) Ask pupils to answer orally, questions 1-5 on the poem (to check recall) without referring to the poem. (exercise 2)

8) Individually or in pairs, pupils complete find the mistakes exercise. (no.3)

9) Individually or in pairs, pupils complete true or false exercise. (no.4)

10) Individually or in pairs, pupils complete fill in the blanks exercise. (no.5)

11) Pupils write their own poem using either one or both homophones (exercise 6 with b) being more challenging!). The poem should be at least 4 lines in length and does not have to rhyme. Invite pupils to read and recite their poem. Pupils then pick one poem they have listened to and write about their favourite moment in it, an exciting character and what they liked about the poem.

Any of the above exercises 3 – 6 could be given as homework exercises.

Answers

4) – 6) Teacher check
7) Exercise 2: 1) arriving late to school; 2) Teacher check; 3) Teacher check; 4) Teacher check; 5) pleased
8) Exercise 3: Correct homophone is on fourth line "But poor Mum had *no* money..."
9) Exercise 4: 1) true; 2) false; 3) true; 4) false
10) Exercise 5: a) know; b) know; c) no; d) no; e) know, no; f) know
11) Exercise 6: Teacher check

Pupils could display their poems on the classroom wall(s).

No, Know

I *know* there is *no* excuse
for my arriving so late
nearly every morning
at the old school gate.

If you *know* Mr.Kelly
who teaches in room ten,
you'll *know* he won't be pleased
when he sees me late again!

I *know* what you're thinking:
no alarm clock to wake you?
*No*body to call you?
Surely you *know* it's not a good
habit for you to be keeping
all the year through!

So what can I do
to arrive here on time?
I *know* I've *no* answer
quite just yet, but perhaps
you could help me to find one
- an easy one I won't forget!

No, Know

Explanation of each word:

No = not a, not one, not any.
Example: I have *no* idea.
No = not at all.
Example: He's *no* stranger to football.

Know = a verb meaning to be certain of a fact.
Example: I *know* that two and two make four.
Know = a verb meaning to be familiar with a person or a thing.
Example: I *know* Michael very well.

Exercise 1

Oral activity

1) Listen to your teacher reading the poem aloud. What do you notice about your teacher's tone of voice? What kinds of gestures and facial expressions is your teacher using?
2) Practise reading the poem aloud. Listen to each reader's tone of voice. Look at the readers' gestures and facial expressions. Are they the same or different?
3) Discuss your reaction to the poem with your teacher and class. What do you like about the poem?

Exercise 2

Oral activity

Questions on the poem:
1) What is the poet's bad habit?
2) What could the poet do to be more punctual?
3) Have you ever been late for school? What was the reason?
4) What happens if you arrive late to school?
5) What word in the poem is a synonym of the word *happy*?

Exercise 3
Reading and Writing activity

Find the mistakes and underline each one. Write the correct word over each incorrect word: (One is correct!)

Jake wanted to buy a pair of rollerblades, but he didn't no where to find them. He asked his friend Tom, but he had know idea. He had know interest in rollerblading. Jake then asked his Mum if she would help him to find some. But poor Mum had no money and said "Son, I no where we can buy a pair of rollerblades, but you'll have to start saving because I have know money to give you right now."

Exercise 4
Reading and Writing activity

True or False:
1) There is no sign on the door. _____
2) Did you no that Dublin is the capital city of Ireland? _____
3) Daragh has no sisters. _____
4) I no where my friend Joe lives. _____

Exercise 5
Reading and Writing activity

Read the poem and see if you can fill in the blanks using *no* or *know*:
a) How do you _____ that Edward is sick?
b) Do you _____ anyone who plays the tin whistle?
c) There are _____ sharks in Ireland.
d) There is _____ need to shout.
e) The children didn't _____ that there was _____ money in the box.
f) I don't think they _____ where he is.

Exercise 6

Writing and Reading activity

1) Write your own poem using either:
a) the word *know* or *no*
or

b) both words *know* and *no*

_____
_____
_____
_____
_____
_____
_____
_____
_____
_____

2) Read and recite your poem to your partner and then to your class.

3) Pick one poem you have listened to and discuss your favourite moment in it. Tell about an exciting character in the poem. Write what you liked about the poem.

_____
_____
_____
_____
_____
_____
_____
_____
_____
_____
_____
_____

Our, Hour

Teachers Notes

Before the lesson

The teacher should have a list of examples and demonstrate how we use gesture, tone of voice and facial expressions in our everyday lives.

The lesson

1) Write the words *our* and *hour* on the whiteboard and elicit knowledge from pupils of each word. Looking at exercise 1, explain to pupils that they are going to listen to you reading aloud a poem called *Our, Hour* and try to recall from the poem the difference in meaning and spelling between each word.

2) Refer pupils to the *Explanation of each word* section at the top of the first activity page for further explanation and examples. Invite pupils to give their own examples.

3) Discuss with the pupils common gestures, tones of voice and facial expressions that we use.

4) Pupils listen to you reading the poem aloud a second time and then discuss your tone of voice, gestures and facial expressions.

5) Individually or in pairs, pupils practise reading the poem aloud and note each reader's tone of voice, gestures and facial expressions.

6) Pupils discuss their reaction to the poem.

7) Ask pupils to answer orally, questions 1-4 on the poem (to check recall) without referring to the poem. (exercise 2)

8) Individually or in pairs, pupils match sentences containing each homophone learned. (exercise 3)

9) Individually or in pairs, pupils complete find the mistakes exercise. (no.4)

10) Individually or in pairs, pupils complete fill in the blanks exercise. (no.5)

11) Pupils write their own poem using either one or both homophones (exercise 6 with b) being more challenging!). The poem should be at least 4 lines in length and does not have to rhyme. Invite pupils to read and recite their poem. Pupils then pick one poem they have listened to and write about their favourite moment in it, an exciting character and what they liked about the poem.

Any of the above exercises 3 – 6 could be given as homework exercises.

Answers

4) – 6) Teacher check

7) Exercise 2: 1) in just under one hour; 2) clean up the mess while waiting for the buns to be cooked; 3) spick and span; 4) Eddie and the poet

8) Exercise 3: a) It takes Mum an hour to get to work. b) I wonder where we're going on our school tour. c) He waited for one whole hour but nobody turned up. d) We put our books back on the shelf. e) I know how many minutes there are in an hour.

9) a) We packed our bags and went to the airport. b) Our journey lasted an hour. c) Our dress rehearsal begins in an hour. d) It took us an hour to make our snowman.

10) a) our; b) hour; c) our; d) Our, hour; e) Our, our; f) our, our

11) Exercise 6: Teacher check

Pupils could display their poems on the classroom wall(s).

Our, Hour

Our homemade chocolate buns
are baking in the oven
and will be ready to eat
in just under one *hour*.

While we are waiting,
let's clean up *our* mess
and in an *hour* or less,
we'll have the kitchen
spick and span
and have saved *our* poor Mum
an *hour* of stress.

The *hour* is up and *our*
buns are ready.
Out of the oven and
onto *our* plates.
One for me and one for Eddie.

Our, Hour

Explanation of each word:

Our = a possessive adjective meaning of or belonging to us.
Example: This is *our* house.

Hour = a noun meaning a period of time amounting to sixty minutes.
Example: It took them one *hour* to get home.

Exercise 1
Oral activity

1) Listen to your teacher reading the poem aloud. What do you notice about your teacher's tone of voice? What kinds of gestures and facial expressions is your teacher using?
2) Practise reading the poem aloud. Listen to each reader's tone of voice. Look at the readers' gestures and facial expressions. Are they the same or different?
3) Discuss your reaction to the poem with your teacher and class. What do you like about the poem?

Exercise 2
Oral activity

Questions on the poem:

1) When will the buns be ready to eat?
2) What good suggestion does the poet make?
3) What words in the poem are synonyms of *clean* and *tidy*?
4) Who gets to eat a chocolate bun?

Exercise 3
Reading and Writing activity

Match the following so that each sentence makes sense:

a) It takes Mum   we're going on our school tour.
b) I wonder where   books back on the shelf.
c) He waited for   there are in an hour.
d) We put our   an hour to get to work.
e) I know how many minutes   one whole hour but nobody turned up.

Exercise 4
Reading and Writing activity

Find the mistakes and rewrite each sentence correctly:

a) We packed hour bags and went to the airport.

_____

_____

b) Hour journey lasted an hour.

_____

_____

c) Our dress rehearsal begins in an our.

_____

_____

d) It took us an hour to make hour snowman.

_____

_____

Exercise 5
Reading and Writing activity

Read the poem and then see if you can fill in the blanks using *our* or *hour*:
a) We lost _____ match against team B.
b) They arrived in Canada an _____ later.
c) Are _____ sandwiches ready yet?
d) _____ teacher told us that the cake would be baked in under an
_____.
e) _____ hair is black and _____ eyes are brown.
f) We can't wait to tell _____ class _____ news.

Exercise 6
Writing and Reading activity

1) Write your own poem using either:
a) the word *our* or *hour*
            or
b) both words *our* and *hour*

_____

_____

_____

_____

_____

_____

_____

_____

_____

2) Read and recite your poem to your partner and then to your class.

3) Pick one poem you have listened to and discuss your favourite moment in it. Tell about an exciting character in the poem. Write what you liked about the poem.

_____

_____

_____

_____

_____

_____

_____

_____

_____

_____

_____

Pair, Pear, Pare

Teachers Notes

Before the lesson

The teacher should have a list of examples and demonstrate how we use gesture, tone of voice and facial expressions in our everyday lives.

The lesson

1) Write the words *pair, pear* and *pare* on the whiteboard and elicit knowledge from pupils of each word. Looking at exercise 1, explain to pupils that they are going to listen to you reading aloud a poem called *Pair, Pear, Pare* and try to recall from the poem the difference in meaning and spelling between each word.

2) Refer pupils to the *Explanation of each word* section at the top of the first activity page for further explanation and examples. Invite pupils to give their own examples.

3) Discuss with the pupils common gestures, tones of voice and facial expressions that we use.

4) Pupils listen to you reading the poem aloud a second time and then discuss your tone of voice, gestures and facial expressions.

5) Individually or in pairs, pupils practise reading the poem aloud and note each reader's tone of voice, gestures and facial expressions.

6) Pupils discuss their reaction to the poem.

7) Individually or in pairs, pupils match sentences containing each homophone learned. (exercise 2)

8) Individually or in pairs, pupils unscramble sentences containing each homophone learned. (exercise 3)

9) Individually or in pairs, pupils complete find the mistakes exercise. (no.4)

10) Pupils write their own sentences including each homophone. (exercise 5)

11) Pupils write their own poem using either one homophone or all three homophones (exercise 6 with b) being more challenging!). The poem should be at least 4 lines in length and does not have to rhyme. Invite pupils to read and recite their poem. Pupils then pick one poem they have listened to and write about their favourite moment in it, an exciting character and what they liked about the poem.

Any of the above exercises 2 – 6 could be given as homework exercises.

Answers

4) – 6) Teacher check

7) Exercise 2: a) Matthew has a new pair of runners. b) Remember to pare your pencil. c) I have a spare pear if you are hungry. d) They had only one pair of socks each. e) I love a pear when it's sweet and juicy.

8) Exercise 3: 1) I will need a sharp pair of scissors to cut through this box. 2) They come in all sorts of flavours like apple and pear. 3) Luke needs to pare his pencil because its nib is very blunt.

9) Exercise 4: a) Mark needs a new pair of glasses. b) Pare it down as carefully as you can. c) Cameron's favourite fruit of all is a pear. d) Thomas bought a new pair of football boots in the summer sales.

10) Exercise 5: Teacher check

11) Exercise 6: Teacher check

Pupils could display their poems on the classroom wall(s).

Pair, Pear, Pare

P a i r is for things that come in twos,

like sunglasses, binoculars

or a *pair* of shiny shoes.

A *pair* of coloured socks,

a *pair* of soft slippers,

a *pair* of gold earrings

or a sharp *pair* of scissors.

P e a r is the name of a fruit

so juicy and sweet

that we all like to eat.

With chocolate flavoured ice-cream,

pear goes down a treat

and tastes just as good

in a tart with a dollop of cream.

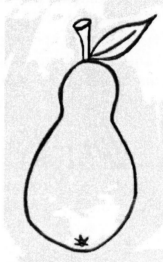

P a r e is another word for

peel or cut, clip or crop,

trim or skin.

May I *pare* my pencil

in this small, yellow bin?

Prepare to *pare* your rosebush

before winter sets in.

Pair, Pear, Pare

Explanation of each word:

Pair = a noun meaning a couple, a match or a combination of two things.
Example: Do you like my new *pair* of shoes?

Pear = a noun meaning a sweet, juicy fruit.
Example: Have an apple or a *pear* as a lunchtime snack.

Pare = a verb meaning to sharpen, cut or clip something which is blunt or overgrown.
Example: Use a pencil sharpener to *pare* your pencil.

Exercise 1
Oral activity

1) Listen to your teacher reading the poem aloud. What do you notice about your teacher's tone of voice? What kinds of gestures and facial expressions is your teacher using?
2) Practise reading the poem aloud. Listen to each reader's tone of voice. Look at the readers' gestures and facial expressions. Are they the same or different?
3) Discuss your reaction to the poem with your teacher and class. What do you like about the poem?

Exercise 2
Reading and Writing activity

Match the following so that each sentence makes sense:

a) Matthew has a new pair   if you are hungry.
b) Remember to pare   of socks each.
c) I have a spare pear   when it's sweet and juicy.
d) They had only one pair   your pencil.
e) I love a pear   of runners.

81

Exercise 3
Writing activity

Can you unscramble the following sentences? (Remember to use a capital letter and full stop or question mark!):

1. a of will cut need I pair through sharp this to scissors box

_____

_____

2. all they flavours pear and come sorts in apple of like

_____

_____

3. nib Luke to pencil because needs his very pare blunt its is

_____

_____

Exercise 4
Reading and Writing activity

Find the mistakes and rewrite each sentence correctly:
a) Mark needs a new pear of glasses.

_____

_____

b) Pair it down as carefully as you can.

_____

_____

c) Cameron's favourite fruit of all is a pare.

_____

_____

d) Thomas bought a new pear of football boots in the summer sales.

_____

_____

Exercise 5
Writing activity

Write your own sentences and include *pair* in the first one, *pear* in the second one and *pare* in the last one:

1. (pair)

_____

_____

2. (pear)

_____

_____

3. (pare)

_____

_____

Exercise 6
Writing and Reading activity

1) Write your own poem using either:
a) the word *pair, pear* or *pare*
or
b) all three words *pair, pear* and *pare*

_____

_____

_____

_____

_____

_____

_____

_____

_____

2) Read and recite your poem to your partner and then to your class.

3) Pick one poem you have listened to and discuss your favourite moment in it. Tell about an exciting character in the poem. Write what you liked about the poem.

_____

_____

_____

_____

_____

_____

_____

_____

_____

_____

Pane, Pain

Teachers Notes

Before the lesson

The teacher should have a list of examples and demonstrate how we use gesture, tone of voice and facial expressions in our everyday lives.

The lesson

1) Write the words *pane* and *pain* on the whiteboard and elicit knowledge from pupils of each word. Looking at exercise 1, explain to pupils that they are going to listen to you reading aloud a poem called *Pane, Pain* and try to recall from the poem the difference in meaning and spelling between each word.

2) Refer pupils to the *Explanation of each word* section at the top of the first activity page for further explanation and examples. Invite pupils to give their own examples.

3) Discuss with the pupils common gestures, tones of voice and facial expressions that we use.

4) Pupils listen to you reading the poem aloud a second time and then discuss your tone of voice, gestures and facial expressions.

5) Individually or in pairs, pupils practise reading the poem aloud and note each reader's tone of voice, gestures and facial expressions.

6) Pupils discuss their reaction to the poem.

7) Ask pupils to answer orally, questions 1 – 5 on the poem (to check recall) without referring to the poem. (exercise 2)

8) Individually or in pairs, pupils unscramble sentences containing each or both homophones learned. (exercise 3)

9) Individually or in pairs, pupils complete true or false exercise. (no.4)

10) Pupils find both homophones in the wordsearch. The words are written either backwards, diagonally, vertically or horizontally. (exercise 5)

11) Pupils write their own poem using either one or both homophones (exercise 6 with b) being more challenging!). The poem should be at least 4 lines in length and does not have to rhyme. Invite pupils to read and recite their poem. Pupils then pick one poem they have listened to and write about their favourite moment in it, an exciting character and what they liked about the poem.

Any of the above exercises 3 – 6 could be given as homework exercises.

Answers

4) – 6) Teacher check

7) Exercise 2: 1) He bumped it off a window pane. 2) He could have looked where he was going. 3) terrible; 4) advice; 5) ease

8) Exercise 3: 1) Please make sure to clean all of the window pane. 2) I know just the thing to cure your pain. 3) James suffered a lot of pain after hitting his head off a window pane.

9) Exercise 4: 1) true; 2) false; 3) true; 4) false

10) Exercise 5:

s	a	h	t	n	e	f
i	*n*	*i*	*a*	*p*	s	t
e	k	w	*a*	v	u	p
n	b	*n*	c	j	l	a
a	*e*	d	*i*	m	o	s
p	q	i	z	*a*	n	e
x	o	y	n	a	*p*	h

11) Exercise 6: Teacher check

Pupils could display their poems on the classroom wall(s).

Pane, Pain

Ted's head ached
with terrible *pain*
after bumping it
off a window *pane*.

On Ted's forehead
there appeared a bump.
Oh the *pain* was pounding,
going thump, thump, thump.

'If only I'd seen
that silly *pane*.
I could have avoided it
with one big jump
and saved myself
this unbearable *pain*.'

An ice-pack helped
to ease Ted's *pain*.
Then some words of advice
came from Mr Kane:
'Look straight ahead at
what's in front of you
and you'll be sure not
to hit a window *pane*!'

Pane, Pain

Explanation of each word:

Pane = a noun meaning a sheet of glass in a window or door.
Example: Look at the fingerprints on my window *pane*.

Pain = a noun meaning an ache or a discomfort in some part of the body.
Example: I have a *pain* in my stomach.

Exercise 1
Oral activity

1) Listen to your teacher reading the poem aloud. What do you notice about your teacher's tone of voice? What kinds of gestures and facial expressions is your teacher using?
2) Practise reading the poem aloud. Listen to each reader's tone of voice. Look at the readers' gestures and facial expressions. Are they the same or different?
3) Discuss your reaction to the poem with your teacher and class. What do you like about the poem?

Exercise 2
Oral activity

Questions on the poem:
1) What caused Ted's head to ache with pain?
2) How could Ted have avoided getting injured?
3) *Severe* and *awful* are synonyms of what word in the poem?
4) *Instruction* and *caution* are synonyms of what word in the poem?
5) *Worsen* and *aggravate* are antonyms of what word in the poem?

Exercise 3

Writing activity

Can you unscramble the following sentences? (Remember to use a capital letter and full stop or question mark!):

1. sure of clean to make please all pane the window

_____

_____

2. just know the I cure to pain your thing

_____

_____

3. hitting James of pane a lot suffered after pain off head his window a

_____

_____

Exercise 4

Reading and Writing activity

True or False:
1) This pane of glass is very dirty._____
2) Jane has a really bad pane in her stomach._____
3) I can't imagine what the pain must have been like._____
4) Make sure that you never play ball near a window pain._____

Exercise 5

Writing activity

The words *pain* and *pane* appear twice in the wordsearch below.
Can you find them?

Write the words here:
1)_____
2)_____
3)_____
4)_____

s	a	h	t	n	e	f
i	n	i	a	p	s	t
e	k	w	a	v	u	p
n	b	n	c	j	l	a
a	e	d	i	m	o	s
p	q	i	z	a	n	e
x	o	y	n	a	p	h

Exercise 6

Writing and Reading activity

1) Write your own poem using either:
a) the word *pane* or *pain*
              or
b) both words *pane* and *pain*

_____

_____

_____

_____

_____

_____

_____

_____

_____

2) Read and recite your poem to your partner and then to your class.

3) Pick one poem you have listened to and discuss your favourite moment in it. Tell about an exciting character in the poem. Write what you liked about the poem.

_____

_____

_____

_____

_____

_____

_____

_____

_____

_____

_____

Peace, Piece

Teachers Notes

Before the lesson

The teacher should have a list of examples and demonstrate how we use gesture, tone of voice and facial expressions in our everyday lives.

The lesson

1) Write the words *peace* and *piece* on the whiteboard and elicit knowledge from pupils of each word. Looking at exercise 1, explain to pupils that they are going to listen to you reading aloud a poem called *Peace, Piece* and try to recall from the poem the difference in meaning and spelling between each word.

2) Refer pupils to the *Explanation of each word* section at the top of the first activity page for further explanation and examples. Invite pupils to give their own examples.

3) Discuss with the pupils common gestures, tones of voice and facial expressions that we use.

4) Pupils listen to you reading the poem aloud a second time and then discuss your tone of voice, gestures and facial expressions.

5) Individually or in pairs, pupils practise reading the poem aloud and note each reader's tone of voice, gestures and facial expressions.

6) Pupils discuss their reaction to the poem.

7) Ask pupils to answer orally, questions 1 – 5 on the poem (to check recall) without referring to the poem. (exercise 2)

8) Individually or in pairs, pupils complete fill in the blanks exercise. (no.3)

9) Individually or in pairs, pupils complete true or false exercise. (no.4)

10) Pupils find both homophones in the wordsearch. The words are written either backwards, diagonally, vertically or horizontally. (exercise 5)

11) Pupils write their own poem using either one or both homophones (exercise 6 with b) being more challenging!). The poem should be at least 4 lines in length and does not have to rhyme. Invite pupils to read and recite their poem. Pupils then pick one poem they have listened to and write about their favourite moment in it, an exciting character and what they liked about the poem.

Any of the above exercises 3 – 6 could be given as homework exercises.

Answers

4) – 6) Teacher check

7) Exercise 2: 1) No noise (...no clattering of spoons or pyrex plates, no noisy machines or screaming voices...); 2) Draw a nice picture on a piece of paper *or* devour a bar of chocolate, one piece after another. 3) Teacher check; 4) piece; 5) bliss

8) Exercise 3: a) piece; b) peace; c) peace; d) piece; e) piece; f) peace

9) Exercise 4: 1) true; 2) false; 3) true; 4) false

10) Exercise 5:

m	o	s	t	a	*p*	y
b	i	j	*e*	d	*i*	i
k	a	g	*c*	*p*	e	a
e	*c*	*a*	*e*	*p*	*c*	z
q	r	*a*	*i*	c	e	e
v	*c*	*i*	*p*	w	u	r
e	n	a	h	f	p	g

11) Exercise 6: Teacher check

Pupils could display their poems on the classroom wall(s).

Peace, Piece

Oh to have a little *peace*.
No clattering of spoons
or pyrex plates!
No noisy machines
or screaming voices!
Just a room filled
with *peace* where
I can sip my tea
and to a *piece* of cake
look forward, like a
lady of leisure
who patiently waits.
There's nothing quite
like some *peace*
and quiet.
Ten minutes of bliss.
Why not try it?
Take one *piece* of paper
and draw a nice picture
or grab a bar of chocolate
and one *piece* after another
quickly devour it.

Peace, Piece

Explanation of each word:

Peace = a noun meaning silence or stillness.
Example: All I ask is that you give me five minutes of *peace*.

Piece = a noun meaning a portion, slice or share of something.
Example: He only had one *piece* of chocolate.

Exercise 1
Oral activity

1) Listen to your teacher reading the poem aloud. What do you notice about your teacher's tone of voice? What kinds of gestures and facial expressions is your teacher using?
2) Practise reading the poem aloud. Listen to each reader's tone of voice. Look at the readers' gestures and facial expressions. Are they the same or different?
3) Discuss your reaction to the poem with your teacher and class. What do you like about the poem?

Exercise 2
Oral activity

Questions on the poem:

1) What is the poet's idea of peace?
2) Name one thing the poet suggests doing in peaceful moments.
3) What is your idea of peace?
4) *Slice* and *sliver* are synonyms of what word in the poem?
5) *Unhappiness* and *misery* are antonyms of what word in the poem?

Exercise 3

Reading and Writing activity

Read the poem and then see if you can fill in the blanks using *peace* or *piece*:
a) May I have one _____ of cheesecake please?
b) All she needed was a few minutes of _____ and quiet.
c) We are all praying for world _____.
d) Johnny wanted to get a _____ of the action.
e) They had one _____ of meat and two scoops of potato.
f) There is great _____ in this village.

Exercise 4

Reading and Writing activity

True or False:
1) I really enjoyed that piece of chocolate._____
2) He's looking forward to an evening of piece._____
3) We wish you all peace and joy this festive season._____
4) Jeremy was only able for one peace of tart._____

Exercise 5

Writing activity

The words *peace* and *piece* appear twice in the wordsearch below. Can you find them?

Write the words here:
1)_____
2)_____
3)_____
4)_____

m	o	s	t	a	p	y
b	i	j	e	d	i	i
k	a	g	c	p	e	a
e	c	a	e	p	c	z
q	r	a	i	c	e	e
v	c	i	p	w	u	r
e	n	a	h	f	p	g

Exercise 6

Writing and Reading activity

1) Write your own poem using either:
a) the word *peace* or *piece*
                    or
b) both words *peace* and *piece*

_____

_____

_____

_____

_____

_____

_____

_____

_____

_____

2) Read and recite your poem to your partner and then to your class.

3) Pick one poem you have listened to and discuss your favourite moment in it. Tell about an exciting character in the poem. Write what you liked about the poem.

_____

_____

_____

_____

_____

_____

_____

_____

_____

_____

Rode, Road

Teachers Notes

Before the lesson

The teacher should have a list of examples and demonstrate how we use gesture, tone of voice and facial expressions in our everyday lives.

The lesson

1) Write the words *rode* and *road* on the whiteboard and elicit knowledge from pupils of each word. Looking at exercise 1, explain to pupils that they are going to listen to you reading aloud a poem called *Rode, Road* and try to recall from the poem the difference in meaning and spelling between each word.

2) Refer pupils to the *Explanation of each word* section at the top of the first activity page for further explanation and examples. Invite pupils to give their own examples.

3) Discuss with the pupils common gestures, tones of voice and facial expressions that we use.

4) Pupils listen to you reading the poem aloud a second time and then discuss your tone of voice, gestures and facial expressions.

5) Individually or in pairs, pupils practise reading the poem aloud and note each reader's tone of voice, gestures and facial expressions.

6) Pupils discuss their reaction to the poem.

7) Ask pupils to answer orally, questions 1 – 5 on the poem (to check recall) without referring to the poem. (exercise 2)

8) Individually or in pairs, pupils match sentences containing each homophone learned. (exercise 3)

9) Pupils write their own sentences including each homophone. (exercise 4)

10) Individually or in pairs, pupils complete find the mistakes exercise. (no.5)

11) Pupils write their own poem using either one or both homophones (exercise 6 with b) being more challenging!). The poem should be at least 4 lines in length and does not have to rhyme. Invite pupils to read and recite their poem. Pupils then pick one poem they have listened to and write about their favourite moment in it, an exciting character and what they liked about the poem.

Any of the above exercises 3 – 6 could be given as homework exercises.

Answers

4) – 6) Teacher check

7) Exercise 2: 1) a toad; 2) They swerved their bikes and rode into a blackberry bush. 3) No; they had only a scratch or two. 4) swerve; 5) a scratch

8) Exercise 3: a) I played with Sam and then we rode to the shop. b) Be careful walking on that road. c) We rode to school every day. d) The road was so icy we were slipping and sliding. e) They saw a huge lorry parked on the side of the road.

9) Exercise 4: Teacher check

10) Exercise 5: Correct homophone is on the fourth line "...was back on the *road* and ...."

11) Exercise 6: Teacher check

Pupils could display their poems on the classroom wall(s).

Rode, Road

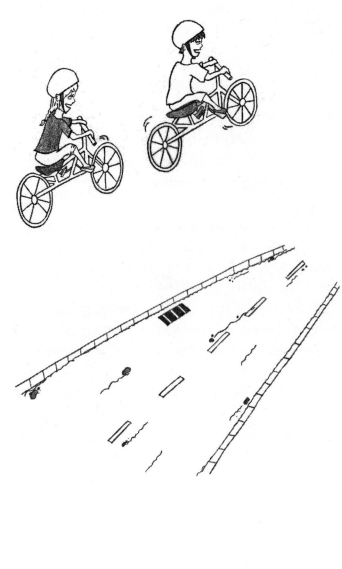

We *rode* our bikes
down a rocky *road*
and nearly lost
our heavy load.

Out jumped a toad
on the rocky *road*
in such a rush that
we swerved our bikes
and into a blackberry
bush we *rode*. Yikes!

Back on our bikes
with a scratch or two
and our heavy load,
we hit the *road*
and *rode* some more
until the rain began to pour.

Rode, Road

Explanation of each word:

Rode = the past tense of the verb *ride*.
Example: They *rode* down a dusty lane.

Road = a noun meaning an open passage whose surface is made of concrete or tarmac.
Example: We drove along a very bumpy *road*.

Exercise 1
Oral activity

1) Listen to your teacher reading the poem aloud. What do you notice about your teacher's tone of voice? What kinds of gestures and facial expressions is your teacher using?
2) Practise reading the poem aloud. Listen to each reader's tone of voice. Look at the readers' gestures and facial expressions. Are they the same or different?
3) Discuss your reaction to the poem with your teacher and class. What do you like about the poem?

Exercise 2
Oral activity

Questions on the poem:
1) What jumped out on the rocky road?
2) What happened next?
3) Were the cyclists seriously hurt? How do you know?
4) What word in the poem is a synonym of *swing, veer* or *turn aside*?
5) What word in the poem is an antonym of *a deep cut*?

Exercise 3

Reading and Writing activity

Match the following so that each sentence makes sense:

a) I played with Sam   every day.
b) Be careful walking   we were slipping and sliding.
c) We rode to school   and then we rode to the shop.
d) The road was so icy   parked on the side of the road.
e) They saw a huge lorry on that road.

Exercise 4

Writing activity

Write your own sentences and include *rode* in the first one, *road* in the second one and both *rode* and *road* in the last one:

1. (rode)

_____

_____

2. (road)

_____

_____

3. (rode, road)

_____

_____

Exercise 5
Reading and Writing activity

Find the mistakes and underline each one. Write the correct word over each incorrect word: (One is correct!)

Jennifer and Jordan road their bicycles down a busy rode. They road in single file and were careful to stay in off the dangerous rode. After a while, Jennifer slowed down and stopped for a break while Jordan road on ahead. Before long, Jennifer was back on the road and quickly caught up with Jordan. They road for another ten minutes before they reached the bakery. Jennifer bought some buns and pastries. Jordan bought some freshly baked bread and then they both road their bicycles home.

Exercise 6
Writing and Reading activity

1) Write your own poem using either:
a) the word *rode* or *road*
                    or
b) both words *rode* and *road*

_____

_____

_____

_____

_____

_____

_____

_____

_____

2) Read and recite your poem to your partner and then to your class.

3) Pick one poem you have listened to and discuss your favourite moment in it. Tell about an exciting character in the poem. Write what you liked about the poem.

_____

_____

_____

_____

_____

_____

_____

_____

_____

_____

Seem, Seam

Teachers Notes

Before the lesson

The teacher should have a list of examples and demonstrate how we use gesture, tone of voice and facial expressions in our everyday lives.

The lesson

1) Write the words *seem* and *seam* on the whiteboard and elicit knowledge from pupils of each word. Looking at exercise 1, explain to pupils that they are going to listen to you reading aloud a poem called *Seem, Seam* and try to recall from the poem the difference in meaning and spelling between each word.

2) Refer pupils to the *Explanation of each word* section at the top of the first activity page for further explanation and examples. Invite pupils to give their own examples.

3) Discuss with the pupils common gestures, tones of voice and facial expressions that we use.

4) Pupils listen to you reading the poem aloud a second time and then discuss your tone of voice, gestures and facial expressions.

5) Individually or in pairs, pupils practise reading the poem aloud and note each reader's tone of voice, gestures and facial expressions.

6) Pupils discuss their reaction to the poem.

7) Individually or in pairs, pupils complete true or false exercise. (no.2)

8) Individually or in pairs, pupils match sentences containing each homophone learned.(exercise 3)

9) Pupils find both homophones in the wordsearch. The words are written either backwards, diagonally, vertically or horizontally. (exercise 4)

10) Pupils write their own sentences including each homophone. (exercise 5)

11) Pupils write their own poem using either one or both homophones (exercise 6 with b) being more challenging!). The poem should be at least 4 lines in length and does not have to rhyme. Invite pupils to read and recite their poem. Pupils then pick one poem they have listened to and write about their favourite moment in it, an exciting character and what they liked about the poem.

Any of the above exercises 2 – 6 could be given as homework exercises.

Answers

4) – 6) Teacher check

7) Exercise 2: 1) true; 2) false; 3) true; 4) false

8) Exercse 3: a) I need help sewing this seam. b) You seem to be going the wrong way. c) They never seem to know where to go next. d) My trouser seam has come undone. e) Don't tell me you've ripped another seam.

9) Exercise 4:

p	m	*m*	*a*	*e*	*s*	b	i
t	*s*	q	r	i	k	*g*	m
m	v	*e*	w	*s*	u	p	e
e	b	f	e	c	o	t	r
e	h	*a*	l	*m*	t	i	a
s	*m*	j	n	d	e	*s*	a
b	e	n	a	s	m	t	u

10) Exercise 5: Teacher check

11) Exercise 6: Teacher check

Pupils could display their poems on the classroom wall(s).

Seem, Seam

You never *seem*
to know when a
seam has come undone.
You walk down a corridor
and there's a laugh
from everyone.

The *seam* on your coat,
the *seam* on your skirt,
the *seam* on your trousers,
the *seam* on your shirt.

And who do we
seem to call on
to *seam* a ripped *seam*?
Our grandmother or mother,
or both as one great team.

Seem, Seam

Explanation of each word:

Seem = a verb meaning to appear to be, look as if or sound like.
Example: You *seem* very happy about it.

Seam = a noun meaning the line along which pieces of fabric are joined by stitching.
Example: She ripped a *seam* on her coat.
Seam = a verb meaning to sew together by a seam.
Example: I will *seam* your shirt.

Exercise 1
Oral activity

1) Listen to your teacher reading the poem aloud. What do you notice about your teacher's tone of voice? What kinds of gestures and facial expressions is your teacher using?
2) Practise reading the poem aloud. Listen to each reader's tone of voice. Look at the readers' gestures and facial expressions. Are they the same or different?
3) Discuss your reaction to the poem with your teacher and class. What do you like about the poem?

Exercise 2
Reading and Writing activity

True or False:
1) You seem to be quite upset._____
2) I never seam to be able to work this properly._____
3) We'll have a seamstress look at your seam._____
4) They all seam a little nervous._____

Exercise 3

Reading and Writing activity

Match the following so that each sentence makes sense:

a) I need help   to know where to go next.
b) You seem to be   ripped another seam.
c) They never seem   sewing this seam.
d) My trouser seam   going the wrong way.
e) Don't tell me you've   has come undone.

Exercise 4

Writing activity

The words *seem* and *seam* appear twice in the wordsearch below. Can you find them?

Write the words here:
1)_____
2)_____
3)_____
4)_____

p	m	m	a	e	s	b	i
t	s	q	r	i	k	g	m
m	v	e	w	s	u	p	e
e	b	f	e	c	o	t	r
e	h	a	l	m	t	i	a
s	m	j	n	d	e	s	a
b	e	n	a	s	m	t	u

Exercise 5
Writing activity

Write your own sentences and include *seem* in the first one, *seam* in the second one and both *seem* and *seam* in the last one:

1. (seem)

_____

_____

2. (seam)

_____

_____

3. (seem, seam)

_____

_____

Exercise 6

Writing and Reading activity

1) Write your own poem using either:
a) the word *seem* or *seam*

or

b) both words *seem* and *seam*

_____

_____

_____

_____

_____

_____

_____

_____

_____

_____

2) Read and recite your poem to your partner and then to your class.

3) Pick one poem you have listened to and discuss your favourite moment in it. Tell about an exciting character in the poem. Write what you liked about the poem.

_____

_____

_____

_____

_____

_____

_____

_____

_____

_____

_____

Stares, Stairs

Teachers Notes

Before the lesson

The teacher should have a list of examples and demonstrate how we use gesture, tone of voice and facial expressions in our everyday lives.

The lesson

1) Write the words *stares* and *stairs* on the whiteboard and elicit knowledge from pupils of each word. Looking at exercise 1, explain to pupils that they are going to listen to you reading aloud a poem called *Stares, Stairs* and try to recall from the poem the difference in meaning and spelling between each word.

2) Refer pupils to the *Explanation of each word* section at the top of the first activity page for further explanation and examples. Invite pupils to give their own examples.

3) Discuss with the pupils common gestures, tones of voice and facial expressions that we use.

4) Pupils listen to you reading the poem aloud a second time and then discuss your tone of voice, gestures and facial expressions.

5) Individually or in pairs, pupils practise reading the poem aloud and note each reader's tone of voice, gestures and facial expressions.

6) Pupils discuss their reaction to the poem.

7) Ask pupils to answer orally, questions 1 – 5 on the poem (to check recall) without referring to the poem. (exercise 2)

8) Individually or in pairs, pupils complete fill in the blanks exercise. (no.3)

9) Individually or in pairs, pupils complete find the mistakes exercise. (no.4)

10) Pupils find both homophones in the wordsearch. The words are written either backwards, diagonally, vertically or horizontally. (exercise 5)

11) Pupils write their own poem using either one or both homophones (exercise 6 with b) being more challenging!). The poem should be at least 4 lines in length and does not have to rhyme. Invite pupils to read and recite their poem. Pupils then pick one poem they have listened to and write about their favourite moment in it, an exciting character and what they liked about the poem.

Any of the above exercises 3 – 6 could be given as homework exercises.

Answers

4) – 6) Teacher check

7) Exercise 2: 1) Mr. Sayers; 2) a large box in one hand and a small bag in the other; 3) cautious, curious; 4) Teacher check (a pair of shoes/slippers etc.) 5) clues

8) Exercise 3: a) stares; b) stairs; c) stares; d) stairs; e) stairs; f) stares

9) Exercise 4: Correct homophone is on the first line "...to come down the *stairs* at once..."

10) Exercise 5:

b	g	s	u	*s*	v	e	r	i	a
i	o	p	t	*e*	q	*s*	k	e	u
j	h	x	f	*r*	*t*	z	q	r	v
t	*s*	*r*	*i*	*a*	*t*	*s*	d	z	c
r	q	m	*i*	*t*	n	j	l	l	f
c	o	r	g	s	t	a	r	e	s
l	*s*	p	e	v	t	s	c	b	d

11) Exercise 6: Teacher check

Pupils could display their poems on the classroom wall(s).

Stares, Stairs

Seven-year-old Stuart
stares down at Mr. Sayers
from the top of the *stairs*.
A large box in one hand
and a small bag in the other,
'You shouldn't have,'
says Stuart's mother who
stares and *stares* at
these gifts from Mr. Sayers.
Stuart decides to walk down
the *stairs* and *stares* some more
at the gifts and Mr. Sayers.
The large box is covered
in red paper with squares
and the small bag is silver,
like Stuart's in under the *stairs*.
'What's in the big box?'
asks Stuart, all *stares*.
'I'll give you two clues,'
says Mr. Sayers.
'They're shiny and bright
and they come in pairs!'

Colour my squares red!

Stares, Stairs

Explanation of each word:

Stares = present tense of the verb *stare* meaning to look at, watch or gaze intensely.
Example: She *stares* at the picture.
Stares = a plural noun meaning fixed gazes.
Example: His *stares* were making us uncomfortable.

Stairs = a noun meaning a set of steps in a building.
Example: I slipped going down the *stairs*.

Exercise 1
Oral activity

1) Listen to your teacher reading the poem aloud. What do you notice about your teacher's tone of voice? What kinds of gestures and facial expressions is your teacher using?
2) Practise reading the poem aloud. Listen to each reader's tone of voice. Look at the readers' gestures and facial expressions. Are they the same or different?
3) Discuss your reaction to the poem with your teacher and class. What do you like about the poem?

Exercise 2
Oral activity

Questions on the poem:
1) Who is Stuart staring at in the poem?
2) What was Mr. Sayers holding?
3) How would you describe Stuart?
4) Name 3 items Mr. Sayers could have had in the big box.
5) *Hints* and *inklings* are synonyms of what word in the poem?

Exercise 3
Reading and Writing activity

Read the poem and then see if you can fill in the blanks using *stares* or *stairs*:
a) He _____ out the window all day long.
b) Poor Jim lost his footing and fell down the _____.
c) The baby _____ at her mother when she is feeding her.
d) We had to walk up three flights of _____ before we reached our hotel room.
e) She never liked hoovering the _____.
f) He _____ at the old man mending the machine.

Exercise 4
Reading and Writing activity

Find the mistakes and underline each one. Write the correct word over each incorrect word. (One is correct!)

Mr. Davis asks his son, Peter, to come down the stairs at once and explain the terrible mess in their front room. Mr. Davis stairs at Peter, waiting for his reply. Peter tries to speak but his Dad's stairs frighten him. "Well, what have you got to say for yourslf, young man?" asks Dad, all stairs. "I am sorry, Dad. We were playing games," replies Peter eventually. Mr. Davis orders Peter to tidy up the mess and finishes by saying "Go back up that stares and do your homework."

117

Exercise 5

Writing activity

The words *stares* and *stairs* appear twice in the wordsearch below. Can you find them?

Write the words here:
1)_____
2)_____
3)_____
4)_____

b	g	s	u	s	v	e	r	i	a
i	o	p	t	e	q	s	k	e	u
j	h	x	f	r	t	z	q	r	v
t	s	r	i	a	t	s	d	z	c
r	q	m	i	t	n	j	l	l	f
c	o	r	g	s	t	a	r	e	s
l	s	p	e	v	t	s	c	b	d

Exercise 6

Writing and Reading activity

1) Write your own poem using either:
a) the word *stares* or *stairs*
                  or
b) both words *stares* and *stairs*

_____

_____

_____

_____

_____

_____

_____

_____

_____

_____

2) Read and recite your poem to your partner and then to your class.

3) Pick one poem you have listened to and discuss your favourite moment in it. Tell about an exciting character in the poem. Write what you liked about the poem.

_____

_____

_____

_____

_____

_____

_____

_____

_____

_____

_____

Steal, Steel

Teachers Notes

Before the lesson

The teacher should have a list of examples and demonstrate how we use gesture, tone of voice and facial expressions in our everyday lives.

The lesson

1) Write the words *steal* and *steel* on the whiteboard and elicit knowledge from pupils of each word. Looking at exercise 1, explain to pupils that they are going to listen to you reading aloud a poem called *Steal, Steel* and try to recall from the poem the difference in meaning and spelling between each word.

2) Refer pupils to the *Explanation of each word* section at the top of the first activity page for further explanation and examples. Invite pupils to give their own examples.

3) Discuss with the pupils common gestures, tones of voice and facial expressions that we use.

4) Pupils listen to you reading the poem aloud a second time and then discuss your tone of voice, gestures and facial expressions.

5) Individually or in pairs, pupils practise reading the poem aloud and note each reader's tone of voice, gestures and facial expressions.

6) Pupils discuss their reaction to the poem.

7) Ask pupils to answer orally, questions 1 – 5 on the poem (to check recall) without referring to the poem. (exercise 2)

8) Individually or in pairs, pupils complete find the mistakes exercise. (no.3)

9) Individually or in pairs, puils complete true or false exercise. (no.4)

10) Pupils find both homophones in the wordsearch. The words are written either backwards, diagonally, vertically or horizontally. (exercise 5)

11) Pupils write their own poem using either one or both homophones (exercise 6 with b) being more challenging!). The poem should be at least 4 lines in length and does not have to rhyme. Invite pupils to read and recite their poem. Pupils then pick one poem they have listened to and write about their favourite moment in it, an exciting character and what they liked about the poem.

Any of the above exercises 3 – 6 could be given as homework exercises.

Answers

4) – 6) Teacher check

7) Exercise 2: 1) The poet dislikes stealing. She would feel unhappy if someone tried to steal from her. 2) She will ignore them and make new friends. 3) Teacher check; 4) friends; 5) belongings

8) Exercise 3: a) You should never steal from anyone. b) Please don't steal my stainless steel cutlery. c) They tried to steal his big steel box to see what was inside. d) Don't you dare steal another slice of cake.

9) Exercise 4: 1) true; 2) false; 3) true; 4) false

10) Exercise 5:

s	d	o	t	*l*	g	p
s	*t*	*e*	*a*	*l*	i	*l*
m	c	*e*	j	h	q	*e*
f	*t*	n	*e*	r	u	*e*
s	k	w	x	*l*	z	*t*
b	v	l	a	i	t	*s*
o	r	t	c	e	l	s

11) Exercise 6: Teacher check

Pupils could display their poems on the classroom wall(s).

Steal, Steel

If you try to *steal*
my new *steel* train,
happy I won't feel
and may not want to
play with you again.

If you try to *steal*
my new *steel* ruler,
ignore you I will
and make new friends
who are much, much cooler.

If you do not *steal*
my new *steel* train
or my new *steel* ruler,
I'll know we have a good
friendship that has no end
and to you, my *steel* belongings
I'd be glad to lend.

Steal, Steel

Explanation of each word:

Steal = a verb meaning to rob or take something from someone without permission.
Example: You tried to *steal* my ipod.

Steel = a noun meaning a silver-coloured, strong, hard metal.
Example: The papers are kept in a big, *steel* box.

Exercise 1

Oral activity

1) Listen to your teacher reading the poem aloud. What do you notice about your teacher's tone of voice? What kinds of gestures and facial expressions is your teacher using?
2) Practise reading the poem aloud. Listen to each reader's tone of voice. Look at the readers' gestures and facial expressions. Are they the same or different?
3) Discuss your reaction to the poem with your teacher and class. What do you like about the poem?

Exercise 2

Oral activity

Questions on the poem:
1) How does the poet feel about stealing?
2) What will the poet do if someone tries to steal her new steel ruler?
3) Have you ever had anything stolen from you? If so, tell what happened and what did you do?
4) The words *enemies* and *foes* are antonyms of what word in the poem?
5) The word *possessions* is a synonym of what word in the poem?

Exercise 3

Reading and Writing activity

Find the mistakes and rewrite each sentence correctly:
a) You should never steel from anyone.

_____

_____

b) Please don't steel my stainless steal cutlery.

_____

_____

c) They tried to steal his big steal box to see what was inside.

_____

_____

d) Don't you dare steel another slice of cake!

_____

_____

Exercise 4

Reading and Writing activity

True or False:
1) I hope you didn't steal anything._____
2) Steal is a silver, shiny metal._____
3) Paperclips are made of steel._____
4) May I steel a moment of your time?_____

Exercise 5

Writing activity

The words *steal* and *steel* appear twice in the wordsearch below.
Can you find them?

Write the words here:
1)_____
2)_____
3)_____
4)_____

s	d	o	t	l	g	p
s	t	e	a	l	i	l
m	c	e	j	h	q	e
f	t	n	e	r	u	e
s	k	w	x	l	z	t
b	v	l	a	i	t	s
o	r	t	c	e	l	s

Exercise 6

Writing and Reading activity

1) Write your own poem using either:
a) the word *steal* or *steel*

or

b) both words *steal* and *steel*

_____
_____
_____
_____
_____
_____
_____
_____
_____
_____

2) Read and recite your poem to your partner and then to your class.

3) Pick one poem you have listened to and discuss your favourite moment in it. Tell about an exciting character in the poem. Write what you liked about the poem.

_____

_____

_____

_____

_____

_____

_____

_____

_____

_____

_____

Tale, Tail

Teachers Notes

Before the lesson

The teacher should have a list of examples and demonstrate how we use gesture, tone of voice and facial expressions in our everyday lives.

The lesson

1) Write the words *tale* and *tail* on the whiteboard and elicit knowledge from pupils of each word. Looking at exercise 1, explain to pupils that they are going to listen to you reading aloud a poem called *Tale, Tail* and try to recall from the poem the difference in meaning and spelling between each word.

2) Refer pupils to the *Explanation of each word* section at the top of the first activity page for further explanation and examples. Invite pupils to give their own examples.

3) Discuss with the pupils common gestures, tones of voice and facial expressions that we use.

4) Pupils listen to you reading the poem aloud a second time and then discuss your tone of voice, gestures and facial expressions.

5) Individually or in pairs, pupils practise reading the poem aloud and note each reader's tone of voice, gestures and facial expressions.

6) Pupils discuss their reaction to the poem.

7) Ask pupils to answer orally, questions 1-5 on the poem (to check recall) without referring to the poem. (exercise 2)

8) Individually or in pairs, pupils complete find the mistakes exercise. (no.3)

9) Pupils find both homophones in the wordsearch. (exercise 4) The words are written either backwards, diagonally, vertically or horizontally.

10) Individually or in pairs, pupils match sentences containing each homophone learned.(exercise 5)

11) Pupils write their own poem using either one or both homophones (exercise 6 with b) being more challenging!). The poem should be at least 4 lines in length and does not have to rhyme. Invite pupils to read and recite their poem. Pupils then pick one poem they have listened to and write about their favourite moment in it, an exciting character and what they liked about the poem.

Any of the above exercises 3 – 6 could be given as homework exercises.

Answers

4) – 6) Teacher check

7) Exercise 2: 1) A dog who lost his tail; 2) He wandered off and lost his way. 3) wandered; 4) scurried; 5) Never go near running machinery.

8) Exercise 3: a) Max the dog has a long, bushy tail. b) Have you another funny tale to tell? c) After hearing the old man's tale, the children went to bed. d) How long is a tiger's tail?

9) Exercise 4:

s	*l*	*i*	*a*	*t*	e	f	p
g	*i*	k	*t*	j	l	*t*	e
o	*a*	b	e	*a*	t	*a*	c
w	*t*	l	v	i	*l*	*l*	e
q	r	p	n	x	t	*e*	m
l	i	e	a	s	p	t	e

10) Exercise 5: a) He was happy to tell us a very old tale. b) A manx cat has no tail. c) A friendly animal always wags its tail. d) She didn't want to hear another sad tale from her friend. e) He made sure to trim its tail.

11) Exercise 6: Teacher check

Pupils could display their poems on the classroom wall(s).

Tale, Tail

I'm here to tell you a little *tale*
about a dog who lost his *tail*.

His name was Rex, his coat was black
and his *tail* so bushy swung over and back.

Rex wandered off one winter's day
and I'm sad to say he lost his way.

As the *tale* goes, he was seen near
a machine for making hay,
wagging his *tail* as he always does.

He got too close to the running machine
and caught his *tail* right in between!

A yelp and a squeal from poor old Rex,
he scurried off in such distress.

Although in pain, I'm glad to say
that soon back home he made his way.
But alas – with an ongoing wail
and without his *tail*.

So now you know my little *tale*
about a dog who lost his *tail*,
can you tell in a couple of words
the moral of this sad, little *tale*?

Tale, Tail

Explanation of each word:

Tale = a noun meaning a story or an account of something.
Example: He lived to tell the *tale*.

Tail = a noun meaning the rear part of a body or thing (for example, an animal or an airplane).
Example: The short *tail* of a rabbit or deer is called a scut.

Exercise 1
Oral activity

1) Listen to your teacher reading the poem aloud. What do you notice about your teacher's tone of voice? What kinds of gestures and facial expressions is your teacher using?
2) Practise reading the poem aloud. Listen to each reader's tone of voice. Look at the readers' gestures and facial expressions. Are they the same or different?
3) Discuss your reaction to the poem with your teacher and class. What do you like about the poem?

Exercise 2
Oral activity

Questions on the poem:

1) What is the poet's tale about?
2) What happened Rex one winter's day?
3) *Ramble* and *roam* are synonyms of what word in the poem?
4) *Amble* and *stroll* are antonyms of what word in the poem?
5) What is the moral of the poem?

Exercise 3
Reading and Writing activity

Find the mistakes and rewrite each sentence correctly:
a) Max the dog has a long, bushy tale.

_____

_____

b) Have you another funny tail to tell?

_____

_____

c) After hearing the old man's tail, the children went to bed.

_____

_____

d) How long is a tiger's tale?

_____

_____

Exercise 4

Writing activity

The words *tale* and *tail* appear twice in the wordsearch below. Can you find them?

Write the words here:
1)_____
2)_____
3)_____
4)_____

s	l	i	a	t	e	f	p
g	i	k	t	j	l	t	e
o	a	b	e	a	t	a	c
w	t	l	v	i	l	l	e
q	r	p	n	x	t	e	m
l	i	e	a	s	p	t	e

Exercise 5

Reading and Writing activity

Match the following so that each sentence makes sense:

a) He was happy to tell us   always wags its tail.
b) A manx cat   its tail.
c) A friendly animal   has no tail.
d) She didn't want to hear   a very old tale.
e) He made sure to trim   another sad tale from her friend.

Exercise 6

Writing and Reading activity

1) Write your own poem using either:
a) the word *tale* or *tail*

or

b) both words *tale* and *tail*

_____

_____

_____

_____

_____

_____

_____

_____

_____

2) Read and recite your poem to your partner and then to your class.

3) Pick one poem you have listened to and discuss your favourite moment in it. Tell about an exciting character in the poem. Write what you liked about the poem.

_____

_____

_____

_____

_____

_____

_____

_____

_____

_____

Team, Teem

Teachers Notes

Before the lesson

The teacher should have a list of examples and demonstrate how we use gesture, tone of voice and facial expressions in our everyday lives.

The lesson

1) Write the words *team* and *teem* on the whiteboard and elicit knowledge from pupils of each word. Looking at exercise 1, explain to pupils that they are going to listen to you reading aloud a poem called *Team, Teem* and try to recall from the poem the difference in meaning and spelling between each word.

2) Refer pupils to the *Explanation of each word* section at the top of the first activity page for further explanation and examples. Invite pupils to give their own examples.

3) Discuss with the pupils common gestures, tones of voice and facial expressions that we use.

4) Pupils listen to you reading the poem aloud a second time and then discuss your tone of voice, gestures and facial expressions.

5) Individually or in pairs, pupils practise reading the poem aloud and note each reader's tone of voice, gestures and facial expressions.

6) Pupils discuss their reaction to the poem.

7) Ask pupils to answer orally, questions 1 – 4 on the poem (to check recall) without referring to the poem. (exercise 2)

8) Individually or in pairs, pupils complete fill in the blanks exercise. (no.3)

9) Pupils write their own sentences including each homophone. (exercise 4)

10) Pupils find both homophones in the wordsearch. The words are written either backwards, diagonally, vertically or horizontally. (exercise 5)

11) Pupils write their own poem using either one or both homophones (exercise 6 with b) being more challenging!). The poem should be at least 4 lines in length and does not have to rhyme. Invite pupils to read and recite their poem. Pupils then pick one poem they have listened to and write about their favourite moment in it, an exciting character and what they liked about the poem.

Any of the above exercises 3 – 6 could be given as homework exercises.

Answers

4) – 6) Teacher check

7) Exercise 2: 1) It won't teem with heavy rain when the team begin to play their game. 2) a soggy pitch; rain-soaked gear; a very wet ball 3) soggy; 4) skill

8) Exercise 3: a) team; b) teem, c) teem; d) team; e) team; f) teem, team

9) Exercise 4: Teacher check

10) Exercise 5:

s	m	i	m	p	t
o	a	a	l	d	u
m	e	e	t	b	f
t	t	q	c	j	g
k	h	n	u	v	m
t	e	e	m	w	t
c	m	g	l	r	y

11) Exercise 6: Teacher check

Pupils could display their poems on the classroom wall(s).

Team, Teem

We hope it won't *teem*
with heavy rain
when the football *team*
start playing their game.
A soggy pitch
and rain-soaked gear.
Slipping and sliding
all over the place
would be for this *team*
a crying shame.
To see and catch
a very wet ball
would be so
hard for this great *team*.
They play with skill
and know every drill.
Please don't *teem* down
and end their dream.

Team, Teem

Explanation of each word:

Team = a noun meaning a group of people working together or a group of players taking part in a sporting competition.
Example: Our *team* won again.

Teem = a verb meaning to pour down heavily.
Example: The rain *teem*ed down last night.

Exercise 1

Oral activity

1) Listen to your teacher reading the poem aloud. What do you notice about your teacher's tone of voice? What kinds of gestures and facial expressions is your teacher using?
2) Practise reading the poem aloud. Listen to each reader's tone of voice. Look at the readers' gestures and facial expressions. Are they the same or different?
3) Discuss your reaction to the poem with your teacher and class. What do you like about the poem?

Exercise 2

Oral activity

Questions on the poem:
1) What is the poet hoping for in the poem?
2) Name three things that would make it difficult for the team to play.
3) *Mushy* and *sopping* are synonyms of what word in the poem?
4) *Inability* and *inexperience* are antonyms of what word in the poem?

Exercise 3
Reading and Writing activity

Read the poem and then see if you can fill in the blanks using either *team* or *teem*:

a) The _____ celebrated another victory on Sunday.

b) The rain began to _____ down at the concert.

c) It's expected to _____ with rain this evening.

d) She really enjoyed being on a winning _____.

e) The senior _____ lost their match.

f) It started to _____ down as the _____ ran onto the pitch.

Exercise 4
Writing activity

Write your own sentences and include *team* in the first one, *teem* in the second one and *team* and *teem* in the last one:

1. (team)

_____

_____

2. (teem)

_____

_____

3. (team, teem)

_____

_____

Exercise 5

Writing activity

The words *team* and *teem* appear twice in the wordsearch below. Can you find them?

Write the words here:
1)_____
2)_____
3)_____
4)_____

s	m	i	m	p	t
o	a	a	l	d	u
m	e	e	t	b	f
t	t	q	c	j	g
k	h	n	u	v	m
t	e	e	m	w	t
c	m	g	l	r	y

<u>*Exercise 6*</u>
Writing and Reading activity

1) Write your own poem using either:
a) the word *team* or *teem*
                or
b) both words *team* and *teem*

_____

_____

_____

_____

_____

_____

_____

_____

_____

2) Read and recite your poem to your partner and then to your class.

3) Pick one poem you have listened to and discuss your favourite moment in it. Tell about an exciting character in the poem. Write what you liked about the poem.

_____

_____

_____

_____

_____

_____

_____

_____

_____

_____

141

Their, They're, There

Teachers Notes

Before the lesson

The teacher should have a list of examples and demonstrate how we use gesture, tone of voice and facial expressions in our everyday lives.

The lesson

1) Write the words *their, they're* and *there* on the whiteboard and elicit knowledge from pupils of each word. Looking at exercise 1, explain to pupils that they are going to listen to you reading aloud a poem called *Their, They're, There* and try to recall from the poem the difference in meaning and spelling between each word.

2) Refer pupils to the *Explanation of each word* section at the top of the first activity page for further explanation and examples. Invite pupils to give their own examples.

3) Discuss with the pupils common gestures, tones of voice and facial expressions that we use.

4) Pupils listen to you reading the poem aloud a second time and then discuss your tone of voice, gestures and facial expressions.

5) Individually or in pairs, pupils practise reading the poem aloud and note each reader's tone of voice, gestures and facial expressions.

6) Pupils discuss their reaction to the poem.

7) Individually or in pairs, pupils complete fill in the blanks exercise. (no.2)

8) Individually or in pairs, pupils complete find the mistakes exercise. (no.3)

9) Pupils write their own sentences including each homophone. (exercise 4)

10) Individually or in pairs, pupils unscramble sentences containing two of the homophones learned.(exercise 5)

11) Pupils write their own poem using either one, two or all three homophones (exercise 6 with b) and c) being more challenging!). The poem should be at least 4 lines in length and does not have to rhyme. Invite pupils to read and recite their poem. Pupils then pick one poem they have listened to and write about their favourite moment in it, an exciting character and what they liked about the poem.

Any of the above exercises 2 – 6 could be given as homework exercises

Answers

4) – 6) Teacher check

7) Exercise 2: a) There; b) their; c) There; d) their, They're; e) there; f) their, They're.

8) Exercise 3: a) Some trees shed their leaves in winter. b) The pupils put their books into their bags. c) They're not going to be able to catch their flight. d) There are eight rooms in their house.

9) Exercise 4: Teacher check

10) Exercise 5: 1) They're over there beside the door. 2) There is a visitor in their classroom. *or* Is there a visitor in their classroom? 3) They're going to eat their lunch now.

11) Exercise 6: Teacher check

Pupils could display their poems on the classroom wall(s).

Their, They're, There

Their, they're, there
you share the same sound
but your spelling and meaning
just spin my head round.

So what could I do
to remember you three?
A difficult job
I'm sure it won't be!

I'll spell out each word
and write out your meaning
and perhaps I'll have remembered
you by teatime this evening.

T h e i r is for anything they own:
their stones, *their* cones, *their* tones, *their* moans.

T h e y apostrophe r e is short for 'they are':
They're not going to get far in that battered, old car.

T h e r e is used to say 'there is' and 'there are' and
also to tell us where something is:
There is one little treat in this bag somewhere and
there are lots more for you in that box over *there*.

Their, They're, There

Explanation of each word:

Their = a possessive adjective meaning of them or belonging to them.
Example: They washed *their* hands.

They're = a contraction of the words *they are*.
Example: *They're* very good at music.

There = a pronoun meaning in that place or position.
Example: I'll be *there* soon.
There = an adverb meaning in, at or to a place.
Example: I'm going *there* on Monday.
There = used as a grammatical subject with verbs like *be*.
Example: *There* is a secret message inside.

Exercise 1
Oral activity

1) Listen to your teacher reading the poem aloud. What do you notice about your teacher's tone of voice? What kinds of gestures and facial expressions is your teacher using?
2) Practise reading the poem aloud. Listen to each reader's tone of voice. Look at the readers' gestures and facial expressions. Are they the same or different?
3) Discuss your reaction to the poem with your teacher and class. What do you like about the poem?

Exercise 2
Reading and Writing activity

Read the poem and then see if you can fill in the blanks using *their, they're* or *there*:
a) _____ are twelve months in a year.
b) The birds build _____ nests in spring.
c) _____ is a lot of chocolate on this cake.
d) The boys and girls are going on _____ school tour today. _____ so excited.
e) Jane said that _____ were lots of things to do in France.
f) After _____ tea, Lucy and Peter are going to bed. _____ very tired.

Exercise 3
Reading and Writing activity

Find the mistakes and rewrite each sentence correctly:

a) Some trees shed there leaves in winter.

_____

_____

b) The pupils put their books into they're bags.

_____

_____

c) They're not going to be able to catch there flight.

_____

_____

d) There are eight rooms in they're house.

_____

_____

Exercise 4

Writing activity

Write your own sentences and include *their* in the first one, *they're* in the second one and *there* in the last one:

1. (their)

_____

_____

2. (they're)

_____

_____

3. (there)

_____

_____

Exercise 5

Writing activity

Can you unscramble the following sentences? (Remember to use a capital letter and full stop or question mark!)

1. beside they're door the there over

_____

_____

2. is there visitor classroom their in a

_____

_____

3. their now lunch to going they're eat

_____

_____

Exercise 6

Writing and Reading activity

1) Write your own poem using either:
a) the word *there, their* or *they're*

or

b) the words *there* and *their* or *there* and *they're*

or

c) all three words *there, their* and *they're*

_____

_____

_____

_____

_____

_____

_____

_____

_____

2) Read and recite your poem to your partner and then to your class.

3) Pick one poem you have listened to and discuss your favourite moment in it. Tell about an exciting character in the poem. Write what you liked about the poem.

_____

_____

_____

_____

_____

_____

_____

_____

_____

_____

Through, Threw

Teachers Notes

Before the lesson

The teacher should have a list of examples and demonstrate how we use gesture, tone of voice and facial expressions in our everyday lives.

The lesson

1) Write the words *through* and *threw* on the whiteboard and elicit knowledge from pupils of each word. Looking at exercise 1, explain to pupils that they are going to listen to you reading aloud a poem called *Through, Threw* and try to recall from the poem the difference in meaning and spelling between each word.

2) Refer pupils to the *Explanation of each word* section at the top of the first activity page for further explanation and examples. Invite pupils to give their own examples.

3) Discuss with the pupils common gestures, tones of voice and facial expressions that we use.

4) Pupils listen to you reading the poem aloud a second time and then discuss your tone of voice, gestures and facial expressions.

5) Individually or in pairs, pupils practise reading the poem aloud and note each reader's tone of voice, gestures and facial expressions.

6) Pupils discuss their reaction to the poem.

7) Ask pupils to answer orally, questions 1-5 on the poem (to check recall) without referring to the poem. (exercise 2)

8) Individually or in pairs, pupils complete true or false exercise. (no.3)

9) Individually or in pairs, pupils complete find the mistakes exercise. (no. 4)

10) Pupils find both homophones in the wordsearch. The words are written either backwards, diagonally, vertically or horizontally. (exercise 5)

11) Pupils write their own poem using either one or both homophones (exercise 6 with b) being more challenging!). The poem should be at least 4 lines in length and does not have to rhyme. Invite pupils to read and recite their poem. Pupils then pick one poem they have listened to and write about their favourite moment in it, an exciting character and what they liked about the poem.

Any of the above exercises 3 – 6 could be given as homework exercises.

Answers

4) – 6) Teacher check

7) Exercise 2: 1) It went straight through the sitting room window. 2) They ran through the front door and threw themselves under Mum's table. 3) patient, understanding; 4) Never to play ball near a window pane; 5) spotted.

8) Exercise 3: 1) true; 2) false; 3) false ; 4) false.

9) Exercise 4: David looked through the local newspaper to see if he could find a photo of his prize-winning art picture. It was nowhere to be seen, so he picked up the paper and threw it in the bin. He went through to the kitchen and asked his Mum to help him surf through the internet to see if he could find his picture. But it wasn't there either. All he could do was wait for his friend to send it through to his phone.

10) Exercise 5:

h	r	t	o	s	g	t	w
a	b	n	h	a	p	r	e
e	e	t	m	r	s	i	r
s	u	o	g	c	e	l	h
c	e	i	t	r	n	w	t
h	g	u	o	r	h	t	a
t	h	r	o	u	g	h	h

11) Exercise 6: Teacher check

Pupils could display their poems on the classroom wall(s).

Through, Threw

Timmy *threw* the ball
to his friend named Jimmy.
But to catch it,
Jimmy was too slow
and it went straight
through the sitting room window.

The boys were so shocked
after hearing the big smash,
they ran *through* the front door
and without even thinking,
threw themselves
under Mum's table -
a good, little hiding place
never used before.

In a little while,
Mum spotted the boys
lying under the table.
She *threw* them a look
of annoyance and sadness,
held out the ball and
asked 'Are you looking for this?'

Out came the boys from
under Mum's table.
To say one word, they were
just not able.
'It's okay,' said Mum.
'Just talk me *through* what
happened outside.
There's no need for you
to run off and hide.'

After telling their story
about the ball going *through*
the window,
the boys *threw* their arms around
Mum and said they regretted it so.
From that day on,
the message was plain:
Timmy and Jimmy were
never to play ball
near a window pane.

Through, Threw

Explanation of each word:

Through = a preposition meaning to go in at one side and come out at the other side of.
Example: We ran *through* the village.

Threw = the past tense of the verb *throw*.
Example: He *threw* the paper in the bin.

Exercise 1

Oral activity

1) Listen to your teacher reading the poem aloud. What do you notice about your teacher's tone of voice? What kinds of gestures and facial expressions is your teacher using?
2) Practise reading the poem aloud. Listen to each reader's tone of voice. Look at the readers' gestures and facial expressions. Are they the same or different?
3) Discuss your reaction to the poem with your teacher and class. What do you like about the poem?

Exercise 2

Oral activity

Questions on the poem:
1) What happened after Jimmy threw the ball?
2) What did the boys do after hearing the big smash?
3) What kind of person was Mum?
4) What lesson did the boys learn?
5) What word in the poem is a synonym of *noticed*?

Exercise 3

Reading and Writing activity

True or False:
1) She walked through the park one sunny day. _____
2) He through it to the captain and he caught it in one hand._____
3) Talk me threw what you did last night. _____
4) We through snowballs at each other all day long. _____

Exercise 4

Reading and Writing activity

Find the mistakes and underline each one. Write the correct word over each incorrect word: (One is correct!)

David looked threw the local newspaper to see if he could find a photo of his prize-winning art picture. It was nowhere to be seen, so he picked up the paper and threw it in the bin. He went threw to the kitchen and asked his Mum to help him surf threw the internet to see if he could find his picture. But it wasn't there either. All he could do was wait for his friend to send it threw to his phone.

Exercise 5

Writing activity

The words *through* and *threw* appear twice in the wordsearch below. Can you find them?

Write each word below:

1) _____

2) _____

3) _____

4) _____

h	r	t	o	s	g	t	w
a	b	n	h	a	p	r	e
e	e	t	m	r	s	i	r
s	u	o	g	c	e	l	h
c	e	i	t	r	n	w	t
h	g	u	o	r	h	t	a
t	h	r	o	u	g	h	h

Exercise 6

Writing and Reading activity

1) Write your own poem using either:

a) the word *through* or *threw*

or

b) both words *through* and *threw*

_____

_____

_____

_____

_____

_____

_____

_____

_____

_____

2) Read and recite your poem to your partner and then to your class.

3) Pick one poem you have listened to and discuss your favourite moment in it. Tell about an exciting character in the poem. Write what you liked about the poem.

_____

_____

_____

_____

_____

_____

_____

_____

_____

_____

_____

To, Two, Too

Teachers Notes

Before the lesson

The teacher should have a list of examples and demonstrate how we use gesture, tone of voice and facial expressions in our everyday lives.

The lesson

1) Write the words *to, two* and *too* on the whiteboard and elicit knowledge from pupils of each word. Looking at exercise 1, explain to pupils that they are going to listen to you reading aloud a poem called *To, Two, Too* and try to recall from the poem the difference in meaning and spelling between each word.

2) Refer pupils to the *Explanation of each word* section at the top of the first activity page for further explanation and examples. Invite pupils to give their own examples.

3) Discuss with the pupils common gestures, tones of voice and facial expressions that we use.

4) Pupils listen to you reading the poem aloud a second time and then discuss your tone of voice, gestures and facial expressions.

5) Individually or in pairs, pupils practise reading the poem aloud and note each reader's tone of voice, gestures and facial expressions.

6) Pupils discuss their reaction to the poem.

7) Individually or in pairs, pupils complete find the mistakes exercise. (no.2)

8) Individually or in pairs, pupils complete fill in the blanks exercise. (no.3)

9) Pupils write their own sentences including each homophone. (exercise 4)

10) Individually or in pairs, pupils match sentences containing each homophone learned.(exercise 5)

11) Pupils write their own poem using either one, two or all three homophones (exercise 6 with b) and c) being more challenging!). The poem should be at least 4 lines in length and does not have to rhyme. Invite pupils to read and recite their poem. Pupils then pick one poem they have listened to and write about their favourite moment in it, an exciting character and what they liked about the poem.

Any of the above exercises 2 – 6 could be given as homework exercises.

Answers

4) – 6) Teacher check

7) Exercise 2: Charlie went to the cinema with his friend named Joe. The two boys had never been to a cinema before. They were really looking forward to their first trip. Mum bought them popcorn instead of ice-cream because the ice-cream was too dear. When they went inside to find a seat, they saw that their classmates, Billy and Jack, were there to watch the film too. They all sat together and had such fun. Charlie would recommend the film to anyone.

8) Exercise 3: a) to; b) two; c) to, too; d) too, to; e) to; f) to, too.

9) Exercise 4: Teacher check

10) Exercise 5: a) Jamie went to school *or* to the swimming pool. b) It was too wet to go out. c) I had two drinks of water. d) Mary said that she would come too. e) I want to go to the swimming pool *or* to school.

11) Exercise 6: Teacher check

Pupils could display their poems on the classroom wall(s).

To, Two, Too

Lucy and Jack
love going *to* school.
From nine till half *two*,
they learn lots from their
teacher and classmates *too*.

The *two* of them
are never *too* tired
to go *to* school
and are oh so good at
obeying every rule.

The *two* little friends
are learning *to* write
numbers one, *two*, three
and their a,b,c.

They listen *to* their teacher
all day long,
when reading a story
and singing a song,
learning new colours,
red, green and blue,
months of the year
and seasons *too*.

To, Two, Too

Explanation of each word:

To = a preposition used to show destination, where someone or something is going.
Example: They ran *to* the bottom of the hill.
To = a preposition placed in front of a verb.
Example: I want *to* walk home.

Two = a cardinal number which is the sum of one and one.
Example: She has *two* brothers.

Too = an adverb meaning as well or also.
Example: Sean is coming *too*.
Too = an adverb meaning extremely.
Example: This brown bread is *too* hard to eat.

Exercise 1
Oral activity

1) Listen to your teacher reading the poem aloud. What do you notice about your teacher's tone of voice? What kinds of gestures and facial expressions is your teacher using?
2) Practise reading the poem aloud. Listen to each reader's tone of voice. Look at the readers' gestures and facial expressions. Are they the same or different?
3) Discuss your reaction to the poem with your teacher and class. What do you like about the poem?

Exercise 2

Reading and Writing activity

Find the mistakes and underline each one. Write the correct word over each incorrect word. (One is correct!)

Charlie went too the cinema with his friend named Joe. The to boys had never been to a cinema before. They were really looking forward too their first trip. Mum bought them popcorn instead of ice-cream because the ice-cream was two dear. When they went inside too find a seat, they saw that their classmates, Billy and Jack, were there two watch the film to. They all sat together and had such fun. Charlie would recommend the film too anyone.

Exercise 3

Reading and Writing activity

Read the poem and then see if you can fill in the blanks using *to, two* or *too*:

a) I love going _____ school.
b) My little nephew is _____ years old.
c) Ann and I are going _____ the shop. Would you like to come _____?
d) The girls were _____ tired _____ walk up the stairs.
e) They wish they knew what _____ do.
f) Robert has been invited _____ the party _____.

Exercise 4
Writing activity

Write your own sentences and include *to* in the first one, *two* in the second one and *too* in the last one:

1. (to)

_____

_____

2. (two)

_____

_____

3. (too)

_____

_____

Exercise 5
Reading and Writing activity

Match the following so that each sentence makes sense:

a) Jamie went   two drinks of water.
b) It was   she would come too.
c) I had   to school.
d) Mary said that   to the swimming pool.
e) I want to go   too wet to go out.

Exercise 6
Writing and Reading activity

1. Write your own poem using either:
    a) the word *to, two* or *too*
        or
    b) the words *to* and *two* or *to* and *too*
        or
    c) all three words *to, two* and *too*

_____

_____

_____

_____

_____

_____

_____

_____

_____

_____

2) Read and recite your poem to your partner and then to your class.

3) Pick one poem you have listened to and discuss your favourite moment in it. Tell about an exciting character in the poem. Write what you liked about the poem.

_____

_____

_____

_____

_____

_____

_____

_____

_____

_____

Week, Weak

Teachers Notes

Before the lesson

The teacher should have a list of examples and demonstrate how we use gesture, tone of voice and facial expressions in our everyday lives.

The lesson

1) Write the words *week* and *weak* on the whiteboard and elicit knowledge from pupils of each word. Looking at exercise 1, explain to pupils that they are going to listen to you reading aloud a poem called *Week, Weak* and try to recall from the poem the difference in meaning and spelling between each word.

2) Refer pupils to the *Explanation of each word* section at the top of the first activity page for further explanation and examples. Invite pupils to give their own examples.

3) Discuss with the pupils common gestures, tones of voice and facial expressions that we use.

4) Pupils listen to you reading the poem aloud a second time and then discuss your tone of voice, gestures and facial expressions.

5) Individually or in pairs, pupils practise reading the poem aloud and note each reader's tone of voice, gestures and facial expressions.

6) Pupils discuss their reaction to the poem.

7) Individually or in pairs, pupils complete fill in the blanks exercise. (no.2)

8) Individually or in pairs, pupils unscramble sentences containing each homophone learned. (exercise 3)

9) Pupils find both homophones in the wordsearch. The words are written either backwards, diagonally, vertically or horizontally. (exercise 4)

10) Individually or in pairs, pupils complete true or false exercise. (no.5)

11) Pupils write their own poem using either one or both homophones (exercise 6 with b) being more challenging!). The poem should be at least 4 lines in length and does not have to rhyme. Invite pupils to read and recite their poem. Pupils then pick one poem they have listened to and write about their favourite moment in it, an exciting character and what they liked about the poem.

Any of the above exercises 2 – 6 could be given as homework exercises.

Answers

4) – 6) Teacher check

7) Exercise 2: a) week; b) weak; c) week; d) weak; e) week; f) weak

8) Exercise 3: 1) There are seven days in a week. 2) The man was so weak he had to lie down. 3) My arms are weak after lifting boxes all week.

9) Exercise 4:

e	t	*k*	o	n	a
a	i	*e*	m	h	p
k	l	*e*	g	o	q
r	b	*w*	*e*	*a*	*k*
s	*w*	*e*	*e*	k	d
p	*k*	*a*	*e*	*w*	e

10) Exercise 5: 1) true; 2) false; 3) true; 4) false

11) Exercise 6: Teacher check

Pupils could display their poems on the classroom wall(s).

Week, Weak

Poor Mr Wilks was feeling
very *weak* all of last *week*.
He could hardly move,
let alone speak.

As *weak* as could be,
he went to his doctor
in the centre of town
for good advice
and medicine to seek.

After checking him thoroughly
up and down,
he said 'It's flu, Mr Wilks,
so it's hot drinks and vitamins
and bed for a *week*.'

After a *week*, Mr Wilks
was feeling a lot less *weak*.
He was so happy he could
move again and once more,
be strong enough to speak.

Week, Weak

Explanation of each word:

Week = a noun meaning a period of seven following days, for example, from Sunday to Saturday.
Example: We spent the *week* in Spain.

Weak = an adjective meaning having no energy, little physical or mental strength.
Example: He was too *weak* to stand up.

Exercise 1
Oral activity

1) Listen to your teacher reading the poem aloud. What do you notice about your teacher's tone of voice? What kinds of gestures and facial expressions is your teacher using?
2) Practise reading the poem aloud. Listen to each reader's tone of voice. Look at the readers' gestures and facial expressions. Are they the same or different?
3) Discuss your reaction to the poem with your teacher and class. What do you like about the poem?

Exercise 2
Reading and Writing activity

Read the poem and then see if you can fill in the blanks using *week* or *weak*:

a) We have P.E. twice a _____.
b) You feel very _____ when you have flu.
c) We're going to the circus next _____.
d) His knee was _____ after the injury.
e) I had to go to the doctor last _____.
f) I am _____. I need to sit down.

<u>Exercise 3</u>

Writing activity

Can you unscramble the following sentences? (Remember to use a capital letter and full stop or question mark!):

1. days a in there week seven are

_____

_____

2. so had man to weak lie was down the he

_____

_____

3. arms weak lifting my after are boxes week all

_____

_____

Exercise 4

Writing activity

The words *week* and *weak* appear twice in the wordsearch below. Can you find them?

Write each word here:
1)_____
2)_____
3)_____
4)_____

e	t	k	o	n	a
a	i	e	m	h	p
k	l	e	g	o	q
r	b	w	e	a	k
s	w	e	e	k	d
p	k	a	e	w	e

Exercise 5

Reading and Writing activity

True or False:
1) The weak animal had to be taken to the vet. _____
2) I play sport every weak. _____
3) We are going to have more snow next week. _____
4) His grandmother was so week, she couldn't speak. _____

<u>*Exercise 6*</u>

Writing and Reading activity

1) Write your own poem using either:
a) the word *week* or *weak*

or

b) both words *week* and *weak*

_____

_____

_____

_____

_____

_____

_____

_____

_____

2) Read and recite your poem to your partner and then to your class.

3) Pick one poem you have listened to and discuss your favourite moment in it. Tell about an exciting character in the poem. Write what you liked about the poem.

_____

_____

_____

_____

_____

_____

_____

_____

_____

_____

_____

Whole, Hole

Teachers Notes

Before the lesson

The teacher should have a list of examples and demonstrate how we use gesture, tone of voice and facial expressions in our everyday lives.

The lesson

1) Write the words *whole* and *hole* on the whiteboard and elicit knowledge from pupils of each word. Looking at exercise 1, explain to pupils that they are going to listen to you reading aloud a poem called *Whole, Hole* and try to recall from the poem the difference in meaning and spelling between each word.

2) Refer pupils to the *Explanation of each word* section at the top of the first activity page for further explanation and examples. Invite pupils to give their own examples.

3) Discuss with the pupils common gestures, tones of voice and facial expressions that we use.

4) Pupils listen to you reading the poem aloud a second time and then discuss your tone of voice, gestures and facial expressions.

5) Individually or in pairs, pupils practise reading the poem aloud and note each reader's tone of voice, gestures and facial expressions.

6) Pupils discuss their reaction to the poem.

7) Ask pupils to answer orally, questions 1 – 5 on the poem (to check recall) without referring to the poem. (exercise 2)

8) Individually or in pairs, pupils match sentences containing each homophone learned. (exercise 3)

9) Pupils write their own sentences including each homophone. (exercise 4)

10) Individually or in pairs, pupils complete find the mistakes exercise. (no.5)

11) Pupils write their own poem using either one or both homophones (exercise 6 with b) being more challenging!). The poem should be at least 4 lines in length and does not have to rhyme. Invite pupils to read and recite their poem. Pupils then pick one poem they have listened to and write about their favourite moment in it, an exciting character and what they liked about the poem.

Any of the above exercises 2 – 6 could be given as homework exercises.

Answers

4) – 6) Teacher check

7) Exercise 2: 1) dark and furry; 2) eager, curious or adventurous; 3) in a field or in a garden; Teacher check 4) tossed; 5) deeper

8) Exercise 3: a) This shop has a whole lot of things for Christmas. b) You have a hole in your jumper. c) They deserve a whole bar of chocolate for their hard work. d) Jamie discovered a big hole in his shoe. e) The whole team were driven to the game by bus.

9) Exercise 4: Teacher check

10) Exercise 5: a) I'm so hungry I could eat one whole pizza. b) The tiny mouse ran down the hole. c) The whole class watched him fall into the hole. d) She waited a whole hour for her to come.

11) Exercise 6: Teacher check

Pupils could display their poems on the classroom wall(s).

Whole, Hole

A dark, furry mole
was seen digging a *hole*
by a *whole* group of children
near a telephone pole.

The *hole* got bigger
as the mole dug deeper
- a *whole* lot of clay
tossed out of the way.

The *whole* group moved closer
for a better view of the mole.
He heard them coming
and darted down the *hole*.

With a *whole* lot less light
down that deep, dark *hole*,
nowhere to be seen
was the dark, furry mole.

Whole, Hole

__Explanation of each word:__

Whole = an adjective meaning total or complete.
Example: He ate a *whole* orange.
Whole = a noun meaning all the parts of a thing.
Example: He has one *whole* and she has one half.

Hole = a noun meaning a gap or an opening in or through something.
Example: There is a *hole* in this bucket.

__Exercise 1__
Oral activity

1) Listen to your teacher reading the poem aloud. What do you notice about your teacher's tone of voice? What kinds of gestures and facial expressions is your teacher using?
2) Practise reading the poem aloud. Listen to each reader's tone of voice. Look at the readers' gestures and facial expressions. Are they the same or different?
3) Discuss your reaction to the poem with your teacher and class. What do you like about the poem?

__Exercise 2__
Oral activity

Questions on the poem:
1) Describe the mole in the poem.
2) What two words would you use to describe the group of children?
3) Where are you most likely to see a mole? Tell about a time when you saw a mole.
4) What word in the poem is a synonym of *hurled* or *thrown*?
5) *Shallower* is an antonym of what word in the poem?

<u>*Exercise 3*</u>
Reading and Writing activity

Match the following so that each sentence makes sense:

a) This shop has a   big hole in his shoe.
b) You have a   whole bar of chocolate for their hard work.
c) They deserve a   were driven to the game by bus.
d) Jamie discovered a   hole in your jumper.
e) The whole team   whole lot of things for Christmas.

<u>*Exercise 4*</u>
Writing activity

Write your own sentences and include *whole* in the first one, *hole* in the second one and both *whole* and *hole* in the last one:

1. (whole)

_____

_____

2. (hole)

_____

_____

3. (whole, hole)

_____

_____

Exercise 5
Reading and Writing activity

Find the mistakes and rewrite each sentence correctly:

a) I'm so hungry I could eat one hole pizza.

_____

_____

b) The tiny mouse ran down the whole.

_____

_____

c) The hole class watched him fall into the hole.

_____

_____

d) She waited a hole hour for her to come.

_____

_____

Exercise 6

Writing and Reading activity

1) Write your own poem using either:
a) the word *whole* or *hole*
                    or
b) both words *whole* and *hole*

_____

_____

_____

_____

_____

_____

_____

_____

_____

2) Read and recite your poem to your partner and then to your class.

3) Pick one poem you have listened to and discuss your favourite moment in it. Tell about an exciting character in the poem. Write what you liked about the poem.

_____

_____

_____

_____

_____

_____

_____

_____

_____

_____

_____

Would, Wood

Teachers Notes

Before the lesson

The teacher should have a list of examples and demonstrate how we use gesture, tone of voice and facial expressions in our everyday lives.

The lesson

1) Write the words *would* and *wood* on the whiteboard and elicit knowledge from pupils of each word. Looking at exercise 1, explain to pupils that they are going to listen to you reading aloud a poem called *Would, Wood* and try to recall from the poem the difference in meaning and spelling between each word.

2) Refer pupils to the *Explanation of each word* section at the top of the first activity page for further explanation and examples. Invite pupils to give their own examples.

3) Discuss with the pupils common gestures, tones of voice and facial expressions that we use.

4) Pupils listen to you reading the poem aloud a second time and then discuss your tone of voice, gestures and facial expressions.

5) Individually or in pairs, pupils practise reading the poem aloud and note each reader's tone of voice, gestures and facial expressions.

6) Pupils discuss their reaction to the poem.

7) Individually or in pairs, pupils complete find the mistakes exercise. (no.2)

8) Pupils find both homophones in the wordsearch. The words are written either backwards, diagonally, vertically or horizontally. (exercise 3)

9) Individually or in pairs, pupils match sentences containing each homophone learned. (exercise 4)

10) Pupils write their own sentences including each homophone. (exercise 5)

11) Pupils write their own poem using either one or both homophones (exercise 6 with b) being more challenging!). The poem should be at least 4 lines in length and does not have to rhyme. Invite pupils to read and recite their poem. Pupils then pick one poem they have listened to and write about their favourite moment in it, an exciting character and what they liked about the poem.

Any of the above exercises 2 – 6 could be given as homework exercises.

Answers

4) – 6) Teacher check

7) Exercise 2: a) Which material would be better? PVC or wood? b) The wood on your sofa is very dark. c) Would you be so kind as to varnish this wood?

8) Exercise 3:

i	b	d	l	u	o	w
e	a	u	s	e	o	l
k	w	q	h	u	p	g
o	o	e	l	c	u	f
o	o	d	o	o	w	x
m	d	j	w	k	t	b

9) Exercise 4: a) What would be a good present for Mum? b) I think that would be a great idea. c) Did you know that wood comes in different colours? d) I would like to know where wood comes from. e) Where would you like to go today?

10) Exercise 5: Teacher check

11) Exercise 6: Teacher check

Pupils could display their poems on the classroom wall(s).

Would, Wood

'*Would* you be able to make
a chair out of *wood*?'
'Make a chair out of *wood*?
Of course I *would*!'
'What *would* you need to make
this chair out of *wood*?'
'What *would* I need?
I *would* need an axe
and a good set of tools,
some varnish and a
measuring tape too.
Some big blocks of *wood*
and a very strong glue.'
'How much time *would* you need
to make this chair out of *wood*?'
'How much time *would* I need?
A couple of days, I *would* say.
Yes, in that time I could.
Once fully varnished
and ready to use,
I *would* be happy to show
you my chair made of *wood*.'

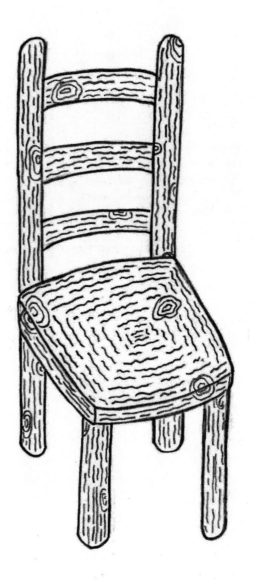

Would, Wood

Explanation of each word:

Would = a verb meaning to show willingness politely.
Example: *Would* you like to play with us?
Would = the past tense of the verb *will*.
Example: She said that she *would* go too.

Wood = a noun meaning a substance of which trees are made.
Example: This frame is made of *wood*.
(**Wood** = a noun meaning a large group of trees.
Example: He searched the *wood* for food.)

Exercise 1

Oral activity

1) Listen to your teacher reading the poem aloud. What do you notice about your teacher's tone of voice? What kinds of gestures and facial expressions is your teacher using?
2) Practise reading the poem aloud. Listen to each reader's tone of voice. Look at the readers' gestures and facial expressions. Are they the same or different?
3) Discuss your reaction to the poem with your teacher and class. What do you like about the poem?

Exercise 2

Reading and Writing activity

Find the mistakes and rewrite each sentence/question correctly:

a) Which material wood be better? PVC or would?

_____

_____

b) The would on your sofa is very dark.

_____

_____

c) Wood you be so kind as to varnish this wood?

_____

_____

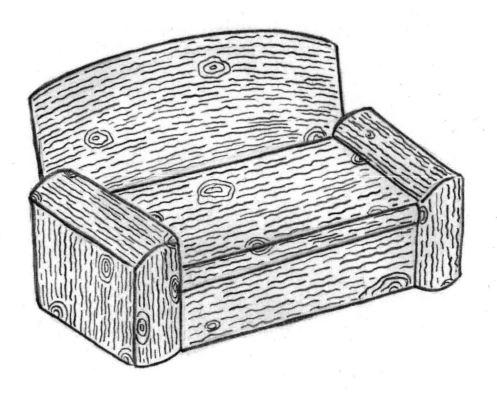

Exercise 3

Writing activity

The words *would* and *wood* appear twice in the wordsearch below. Can you find them?

Write the words here:
1)_____
2)_____
3)_____
4)_____

i	b	d	l	u	o	w
e	a	u	s	e	o	l
k	w	q	h	u	p	g
o	o	e	l	c	u	f
o	o	d	o	o	w	x
m	d	j	w	k	t	b

Exercise 4

Reading and Writing activity

Match the following so that each sentence makes sense:

a) What would be
b) I think that
c) Did you know that
d) I would like to know
e) Where would

wood comes in different colours?
would be a great idea.
a good present for Mum?
you like to go today?
where wood comes from.

Exercise 5

Writing activity

Write your own sentences and include *would* in the first one, *wood* in the second one and *would* and *wood* in the last one:

1. (would)

_____

_____

2. (wood)

_____

_____

3. (would, wood)

_____

_____

Exercise 6

Writing and Reading activity

1) Write your own poem using either:
a) the word *would* or *wood*
or
b) both words *would* and *wood*

_____

_____

_____

_____

_____

_____

_____

_____

_____

2) Read and recite your poem to your partner and then to your class.

3) Pick one poem you have listened to and discuss your favourite moment in it. Tell about an exciting character in the poem. Write what you liked about the poem.

_____

_____

_____

_____

_____

_____

_____

_____

_____

_____

Write, Right

Teachers Notes

Before the lesson

The teacher should have a list of examples and demonstrate how we use gesture, tone of voice and facial expressions in our everyday lives.

The lesson

1) Write the words *write* and *right* on the whiteboard and elicit knowledge from pupils of each word. Looking at exercise 1, explain to pupils that they are going to listen to you reading aloud a poem called *Write, Right* and try to recall from the poem the difference in meaning and spelling between each word.

2) Refer pupils to the *Explanation of each word* section at the top of the first activity page for further explanation and examples. Invite pupils to give their own examples.

3) Discuss with the pupils common gestures, tones of voice and facial expressions that we use.

4) Pupils listen to you reading the poem aloud a second time and then discuss your tone of voice, gestures and facial expressions.

5) Individually or in pairs, pupils practise reading the poem aloud and note each reader's tone of voice, gestures and facial expressions.

6) Pupils discuss their reaction to the poem.

7) Individually or in pairs, pupils complete fill in the blanks exercise. (no.2)

8) Individually or in pairs, pupils unscramble sentences containing both homophones learned. (exercise 3)

9) Pupils find both homophones in the wordsearch. The words are written either backwards, diagonally, vertically or horizontally. (exercise 4)

10) Individually or in pairs, pupils complete true or false exercise. (no. 5)

11) Pupils write their own poem using either one or both homophones (exercise 6 with b) being more challenging!). The poem should be at least 4 lines in length and does not have to rhyme. Invite pupils to read and recite their poem. Pupils then pick one poem they have listened to and write about their favourite moment in it, an exciting character and what they liked about the poem.

Any of the above exercises 2 – 6 could be given as homework exercises.

Answers

4) – 6) Teacher check

7) Exercise 2: a) write; b) right; c) right; d) Write; e) right, write; f) right.

8) Exercise 3: 1) Write about what happened in the story in your own words. 2) This is not the right time to be playing tricks. 3) Please write your name on the right side of the page.

9) Exercise 4:

e	*t*	*h*	*g*	*i*	*r*	t
s	u	f	o	w	a	p
p	l	m	n	*t*	s	i
c	*e*	b	*h*	w	k	b
d	*t*	*g*	v	*r*	f	e
i	*i*	x	r	*i*	a	m
r	*r*	j	q	*t*	r	w
t	*w*	z	e	*e*	w	d

10) Exercise 5: 1) true; 2) false; 3) true; 4) false.

11) Exercise 6: Teacher check

Pupils could display their poems on the classroom wall(s).

Write, Right

If a story about Rory
I decide to *write*,
will you please check
if my spelling is *right*?

If a get better letter
I decide to *write*,
will you please check
if my layout is *right*?

If ten Christmas words
you ask me to *write*,
where on my copy do
I need to start -
the left side or *right*?

If I *write* out my tables
and learn them every night,
do you think there's a chance
that in my Friday morning test,
I'll get them all *right*?

Write, Right

Explanation of each word:

Write = a verb meaning to mark or draw words, numbers or symbols on a surface with a pencil, pen, etc.
Example: Please *write* your name here.

Right = an adjective meaning correct or true.
Example: I got the *right* answer.
Right = an adjective meaning suitable or proper.
Example: You are the *right* person to do this.
Right = an adjective meaning of or located on the right, the opposite of left.
Example: Do I need to turn left or *right*?

Exercise 1
Oral activity

1) Listen to your teacher reading the poem aloud. What do you notice about your teacher's tone of voice? What kinds of gestures and facial expressions is your teacher using?
2) Practise reading the poem aloud. Listen to each reader's tone of voice. Look at the readers' gestures and facial expressions. Are they the same or different?
3) Discuss your reaction to the poem with your teacher and class. What do you like about the poem?

Exercise 2

Reading and Writing activity

Read the poem and then see if you can fill in the blanks using *write* or *right*:

a) I must _____ a letter to my penfriend.

b) How many answers did I get _____?

c) Remember to walk on the _____ side of the corridor.

d) _____ down four things you know about Autumn.

e) You are so _____. I should _____ it all down on paper first.

f) This is the _____ way to do it.

Exercise 3

Writing activity

Can you unscramble the following sentences? (Remember to use a capital letter and full stop or question mark!):

1. own in story the what your write happened about words in

_____

_____

2. be time is playing right to this tricks the not

_____

_____

3. name side on please right of your the write page the

_____

_____

Exercise 4

Writing activity

The words *write* and *right* appear twice in the wordsearch below. Can you find them?

Write the words here:
1)_____
2)_____
3)_____
4)_____

e	t	h	g	i	r	t
s	u	f	o	w	a	p
p	l	m	n	t	s	i
c	e	b	h	w	k	b
d	t	g	v	r	f	e
i	i	x	r	i	a	m
r	r	j	q	t	r	w
t	w	z	e	e	w	d

Exercise 5

Reading and Writing activity

True or False:
1) You got 18 right out of 20._____
2) Right a story about a camping trip with your family._____
3) It's a lovely coat but it's not the right size._____
4) The boys stood on the left and the girls stood on the write._____

Exercise 6

Writing and Reading activity

1) Write your own poem using either:

a) the word *write* or *right*

or

b) both words *write* and *right*

_____

_____

_____

_____

_____

_____

_____

_____

_____

2) Read and recite your poem to your partner and then to your class.

3) Pick one poem you have listened to and discuss your favourite moment in it. Tell about an exciting character in the poem. Write what you liked about the poem.

_____

_____

_____

_____

_____

_____

_____

_____

_____

_____

Your, You're

Teachers Notes

Before the lesson

The teacher should have a list of examples and demonstrate how we use gesture, tone of voice and facial expressions in our everyday lives.

The lesson

1) Write the words *your* and *you're* on the whiteboard and elicit knowledge from pupils of each word. Looking at exercise 1, explain to pupils that they are going to listen to you reading aloud a poem called *Your, You're* and try to recall from the poem the difference in meaning and spelling between each word.

2) Refer pupils to the *Explanation of each word* section at the top of the first activity page for further explanation and examples. Invite pupils to give their own examples.

3) Discuss with the pupils common gestures, tones of voice and facial expressions that we use.

4) Pupils listen to you reading the poem aloud a second time and then discuss your tone of voice, gestures and facial expressions.

5) Individually or in pairs, pupils practise reading the poem aloud and note each reader's tone of voice, gestures and facial expressions.

6) Pupils discuss their reaction to the poem.

7) Ask pupils to answer orally, questions 1 – 5 on the poem (to check recall) without referring to the poem. (exercise 2)

8) Individually or in pairs, pupils complete find the mistakes exercise. (no.3)

9) Individually or in pairs, pupils complete fill in the blanks exercise. (no.4)

10) Individually or in pairs, pupils match sentences containing each homophone learned. (exercise 5)

11) Pupils write their own poem using either one or both homophones (exercise 6 with b) being more challenging!). The poem should be at least 4 lines in length and does not have to rhyme. Invite pupils to read and recite their poem. Pupils then pick one poem they have listened to and write about their favourite moment in it, an exciting character and what they liked about the poem.

Any of the above exercises 3 – 6 could be given as homework exercises.

Answers

4) – 6) Teacher check

7) Exercise 2: 1) Susie; 2) fearless; likes animals; She's not afraid of the mouse. 3) Teacher check 4) trembling; 5) harmless

8) Exercise 3: Correct homophone is on the first line "*You're* so good at music."

9) Exercise 4: a) your; b) You're; c) You're; d) you're; e) Your; f) You're, your

10) Exercise 5: a) I know you're going to be just fine. b) There's a spider on your jumper. c) She knows where your friend lives. d) They all think you're the right person to be captain. e) I do hope that your sister is feeling better.

11) Exercise 6: Teacher check

Pupils could display their poems on the classroom wall(s).

Your, You're

You're on *your* way
to *your* granny's house
when *your* sister Susie
sees a small, grey mouse.

You're suddenly shaking
with the fright,
hoping the scary creature
will not bite.

Your body's trembling,
you're sweating too.
Your sister Susie
starts laughing at you.

'Don't tell me *you're*
afraid of a small, grey mouse!
He's a harmless little soul
that lives in a hole,
much, much smaller
than *your* own house!'

Your, You're

Explanation of each word:

Your = a possessive adjective meaning belonging to you or of you.
Example: Remember to brush *your* teeth.

You're = a contraction of the words *you are*.
Example: *You're* not the only one.

Exercise 1
Oral activity

1) Listen to your teacher reading the poem aloud. What do you notice about your teacher's tone of voice? What kinds of gestures and facial expressions is your teacher using?
2) Practise reading the poem aloud. Listen to each reader's tone of voice. Look at the readers' gestures and facial expressions. Are they the same or different?
3) Discuss your reaction to the poem with your teacher and class. What do you like about the poem?

Exercise 2
Oral activity

Questions on the poem:

1) What name is given to the sister in the poem?
2) What words would you use to describe Susie? Why?
3) Have you ever seen a mouse before? How did you react?
4) *Shaking* is a synonym of what word in the poem?
5) *Dangerous* is an antonym of what word in the poem?

Exercise 3

Reading and Writing activity

Find the mistakes and underline each one. Write the correct word over each incorrect word: (one is correct!)

You're so good at music. Your just the person we need to play the lead role in our school musical. You're teacher has told me that you're singing voice is amazing and that you're dancing ability is excellent. Now, I'm sure your aware that your going to have to practise many long hours right up until you're first performance. You're teacher has also mentioned that as well as you're talent for music, your a very hard worker, so I think your well able for this task. You're school and family will be very proud of you.

Exercise 4
Reading and Writing activity

Read the poem and then see if you can fill in the blanks using *your* or *you're*:

a) Ben, where are _____ football boots?

b) _____ going to have to wear a raincoat today.

c) _____ not the only one.

d) I think _____ making a big mistake.

e) _____ reading has much improved.

f) _____ sitting quietly listening to _____ music.

Exercise 5
Reading and Writing activity

Match the following so that each sentence makes sense:

a) I know you're   your friend lives.

b) There's a spider   you're the right person to be captain.

c) She knows where   going to be just fine.

d) They all think   your sister is feeling better.

e) I do hope that   on your jumper.

Exercise 6

Writing and Reading activity

1) Write your own poem using either:
a) the word *your* or *you're*

or

b) both words *your* and *you're*

_____

_____

_____

_____

_____

_____

_____

_____

_____

2) Read and recite your poem to your partner and then to your class.

3) Pick one poem you have listened to and discuss your favourite moment in it. Tell about an exciting character in the poem. Write what you liked about the poem.

_____

_____

_____

_____

_____

_____

_____

_____

_____

_____